Ground Force
Weekend Workbook

Consultant Editor: Alan Titchmarsh
Garden designs: Alan Titchmarsh
Written by Steve Bradley

BBC

This book is published to accompany the television
series entitled Ground Force, which was first broadcast
in 1997. The series was produced by Bazal Productions
(a GMG Endemol Entertainment Company) for
BBC Television.
Executive Producer: Carol Haslam
Producer/director: John Thornicroft

Published by BBC Worldwide Limited, Woodlands,
80 Wood Lane, London W12 0TT

First published 1999
Reprinted 1999, (five times), 2000 (three times)

ISBN 0 563 38452 2

Commissioning Editor: Nicky Copeland
Project Editor: Khadija Manjlai
Copy-editor: Richard Rosenfeld
Picture Researcher: Susanna Parker
Art Editor and Designer: Town Group Creative
Illustrator : Amanda Patton

Set in MyriadMM and AGaramond
Printed and bound in France by Imprimerie Pollina s.a.
Colour separations by Imprimerie Pollina s.a.
Cover printed by Imprimerie Pollina s.a.

contents

THE *GROUND FORCE* TEAM

It may seem like a dream come true to have your garden turned from an unsightly, overgrown plot into a beautifully designed and finished oasis in just two days (and for the lucky few who have appeared on *Ground Force*, it was), but you don't have to wait for the *Ground Force* team to come knocking at your door. You can make a similar transformation yourself. To create the perfect garden, you don't need to be a trained horticulturist or an experienced builder. The real secret is careful planning and a little imagination, as this book shows. While you may not have Alan, Charlie and Tommy with you in person, the *Weekend Workbook* is the perfect substitute.

Tommy 'Two-days' Walsh, as he has come to be known, runs his own small building business in Hackney, East London, which specializes in hard landscaping, the part of gardening that doesn't involve the planting. On leaving school, he worked with his father, who manufactured garden products and carried out hard landscaping. Tommy met the executive producer of *Ground Force*, Carol Haslam, while he was doing building work on her house. She invited him to take part in a screen test with Charlie Dimmock and they were subsequently invited to join the Force. Tommy's no-nonsense approach to clearing, levelling and building has encouraged people all over the country to tackle these tasks for themselves.

Alan Titchmarsh started as an apprentice gardener at a local nursery in Yorkshire and then attended agricultural college before becoming a student at the Royal Botanic Gardens, Kew, where he was awarded the Kew Diploma. Twice named Gardening Writer of the Year, Alan is now author of over thirty gardening books and a regular contributor to BBC *Gardeners' World Magazine*, *Radio Times* and the *Daily Mail*.

Popular on television and radio as a gardening expert and presenter, Alan has fronted programmes as diverse as *Points of View*, *Pebble Mill*, *Songs of Praise*, *Titchmarsh's Travels* and the *Chelsea Flower Show*.

In 1997 he was named Yorkshire Man of the Year and Television Broadcaster of the Year by the Garden Writers Guild. He currently presents BBC2's *Gardeners' World*. His first novel, *Mr MacGregor*, the story of the life and loves of a TV gardener, was published in 1998.

Alan designs the *Ground Force* gardens, shaping the owners' aspirations into achievable plans before helping to turn them into reality while keeping a close eye on the clock. He also gets his hands and knees dirty.

Charlie Dimmock is a trained horticulturist who specializes in water features. She is gardener at a water garden centre in Romsey, Hampshire, and manages the shop. Charlie trained as an amenity horticulturist in Winchester and Somerset, and spent a year of her training at the Chelsea Physic Garden, London. She was discovered by the producer/director of *Ground Force*, John Thornicroft, who had met her five years previously when she built a pond for the Meridian TV series *Grass Roots*.

Charlie is the plantswoman on the series, but her willingness to tackle much of the heavy work has endeared her to viewers and Force-mates alike.

DESIGN BASICS

Designing a garden sounds complicated, but it couldn't be easier and it's incredible fun. You can have virtually anything you like – a black and white garden, all pinks and blues, the gentle, chic or innovative – simply follow the basic rules overleaf.

turning over a
NEW LEAF

Whether you have lived in your house for a while or you've recently moved in and re-decorated your new home, you will need to think about tackling your garden at some stage. You may not have the *Ground Force* team to help you make it over in two days, but you can certainly achieve the same results with the help of this book…and a little hard work.

WHAT DO YOU WANT?

As with any garden that the *Ground Force* team tackles, the first thing you need to think about is what you want to use your garden for and what you'd like in it. You might consider making it Japanese, Mediterranean, all green or all white; totally screen out the neighbours; get rid of the grass and have decking instead; have areas of wide open space with everything immediately obvious and then contrasting, separate sections; you can have rockeries, running water,

still water, fountains and waterfalls, play areas and barbecues – anything that takes your fancy.

Before you start, get as many ideas as you can by looking through magazines and visiting gardens – the great, the good, the romantic, the modern. The more gardens you see, the better. Make lists of plants that catch your eye and, if you find an interesting feature, adapt and scale down what you see to suit your own garden. For example, instead of a sensational laburnum tunnel, you could have one single tree, with red tulips and white honesty planted round the base in spring followed by big, bold purple alliums. And a futuristic, modernist feel could be injected into a small area with structural plants such as euphorbia and grasses with long, twisty metal rods painted in bright colours spearing out of the ground.

You should also think about whether you need to make over your entire garden all in one go or in stages, or perhaps revamp just a small part of it. Whatever you decide, you must have an overall design in mind.

THE WISHLIST CHECKLIST

Your list of requirements to transform your neglected plot into your dream garden may seem never-ending, but don't worry, the following points will help you to shape and trim it.

Budget – Decide on a realistic budget and stick to it. Work out whether you'll need paid help for some jobs. Remember that the cost of materials, plants and hire equipment can soon add up.

Length of stay – If you're planning to stay in your home a while, you can afford to wait for your garden to mature. If you want a more 'instant' garden, it'll cost you more. Plan this into your budget.

Safety – If you have babies or young children, you won't want a water feature or any poisonous plants. Think about slopes and moving around the garden if an elderly person lives with you.

Level of maintenance – Are you a lazy or keen gardener? It makes a difference to the design of your garden. If you're

Gardens can be designed to suit particular needs. Paths were important in this one. They had to be wide enough for wheelchair access and provide a suitable surface on which to race model cars.

the former, opt for low-maintenance features, such as ground-cover plants or mulch, to save regular weeding rather than masses of annuals in a border, which need a lot of looking after.

WHAT DO YOU HAVE?

The next thing you need to do is to look at what already exists in your garden and think about how it can be re-used. It can be tempting, especially if you're revamping your whole garden, to throw everything out and start with a clean slate, but this could be a costly mistake.

Note down the size and shape of your garden. Consider the sunny and shady parts (to help you position sitting areas and arrange sun- and shade-loving plants), and then make a list of all the trees, shrubs, plants, and features such as sheds, ponds and patios. Divide this list into three categories: the must keep, the maybes and the must go.

The must keep category could apply equally to structures that are well past their best. A patio with a worn surface, for example, could easily become the foundation for a smart new wooden deck. An old wall could become a new path, and discarded timber makes excellent shuttering for containing the concrete for pathways, the base for a shed or greenhouse. Any small pieces of scrap wood you can pull away can be cut for wooden pegs for marking out and setting ground levels (see pages 18–19).

Since new plants, especially large mature ones, can be very expensive, keep as many old ones as you can. If you can spare a year before doing up a new garden, take photographs every month. Remember what is there and detail all the key information: the flowering time, colour, berries, foliage (especially any autumn colour change).

It may be that the right plants are there, but they are struggling to survive because they are in the wrong places (see pages 32–35). By simply moving them to a different part of the garden, a lacklustre specimen can be transformed into a healthy, attractive plant in a few seasons. Remember, bulbs basically lie dormant underground until the conditions are right, whereupon they flower, store energy for next year's display, die back and vanish. It therefore pays to delay digging everything up until you've spent at least one spring in the garden. Put large pebbles round the bulbs so that you don't dig them up. Don't use sticks as they always disappear.

Above Ring the changes, while sustaining the illusion of maturity, by combining new plants with those already established. Growing climbers to cover walls helps remove the newness of a garden very quickly.

Left Keep plants with a low, spreading habit as they are perfect for softening the straight lines and hard edges of paths and other garden structures.

DESIGNS
on your garden

Making a plan is the easiest way of putting all your ideas down on paper. It helps you become more focused and allows you to change your mind with just an eraser.

THE MASTER PLAN

There are several advantages to working with a plan. It highlights the number and position of key features and makes it easier to see whether they gel or link properly. You'll quickly be able to see if the garden is lop-sided, with large areas where nothing happens adjoining a section where it becomes chaotic. A plan also provides a checklist, making sure nothing is forgotten. Obvious things can get missed and, after the next stage, it might be too late.

The plan does not have to be an intricate, mathematically precise work of art, just a basic outline. All that matters is that you can understand it, and that the shape and dimensions, the slopes and depressions, and essential features such as clothes lines are clearly marked. The bigger the drawing, the better.

MEASURING AND LAYOUT

Before you can start on your masterplan, you need to draw a scaled layout of the existing garden. It's not as difficult as it sounds. Basically you need two people and a measuring tape. You also need to record any significant changes in level in case you are going to build a flight of steps or change the slope of the garden.

This measuring and planning stage is highly important when designing any garden, but it takes on extra value when some areas take many years to develop as it gives a constant reference. It will also be invaluable for tackling future projects and, best of all, helps identify all those plants whose labels get torn off or lost. Even though the *Ground Force* team isn't seen to go through this process, Alan is given measurements, and while he skips straight to drawing out the final plan you will need a scaled layout. Remember, Alan's been designing gardens for years, while this might be your first.

SIMPLE, ACCURATE MEASURING

First measure the rear of the house. Hold the tape measure and read off the measurements of such things as

A long, thin garden can be made to seem wider than it is by having a curved path. Sectioning the garden into distinct areas also helps to break up its length.

manholes, drains, the corners of the house, etc. until you have measurements for the whole width of the garden. Do the same down the length of the garden. Remember to include the measurements and positions of any trees, shed, greenhouse, patio and so on.

IRREGULAR SHAPES

Measuring and accurately drawing regular shapes, such as circles, squares, rectangles and triangles, is easy. But what happens if your garden boundaries, like many, are all

Create the illusion of length in a short, wide garden by running a diagonal axis across the area.

wiggles and curves? The solution is remarkably straightforward. Divide the entire area into smaller areas with fixed shapes whose dimensions you can easily plot. Add your measurements to your plan.

ON TO PAPER

Once you've measured every conceivable part of your plot, take a sheet of graph paper and decide on a scale, say, 2 sq cm to represent 1 sq m. Then transfer the measurements on to paper to create your masterplan. The bigger the drawing, the better. Take plenty of photocopies of the master. No one gets it right first time, or the second.

DESIGN BASICS

You're almost ready to begin positioning your features, but before you start, it's worth spending a few minutes thinking about a couple of design essentials.

 The size and shape of your garden will have an effect on what you can do with it. Long, thin gardens could be broken into a series of rooms with a seating area adjoining the house, a planting area or lawn, and an area for a shed or compost heap. Connect the areas with an S-shaped path down the middle (as the *Ground Force* team did with another of the gardens (see plan opposite) and have screens or posts to section off the areas. If you have a square garden with a nice view, put planting or a path leading to it, or

have a circular lawn with borders around it to break up the shape. Even a small garden can be made to look bigger by having a lot of planting. It sounds odd, but it's true.

 Make the design of your garden as simple as you can. It can look cluttered if you try to include too many separate elements and the more complicated it is, the more maintenance it's going to need. Simplify things by co-ordinating the colour of materials with the house or each other. For example, a patio and a retaining wall could both be made of yellow brick.

 Always take into account who is going to use the garden and at which time of the day. If you use the garden mostly when you get home after work, place the patio area where you will catch the evening sun. If there are children, have the play area near the house, where you can keep an eye on them, with the elegant, formal areas furthest away.

New houses, new dimensions

New properties, especially when part of a development, often have scaled plans of the gardens already drawn up. Check with the builder's site office and the estate agent. These plans save a lot of time and will have been done by experts.

getting your ideas
DOWN ON
PAPER

At last, you're ready to start sketching out your dream garden. Take your time drawing your plan. You'll go through several different versions before you arrive at your final one and don't be despondent if it doesn't look as beautiful as Alan's plan. Remember it's only to help you and there's no need to use colour if you don't want to.

MAKING THE GARDEN YOUR OWN

Planning your own garden is all about creating a space that suits you: your style, personality and way of life. As you start to position the features from your wishlist on the masterplan, you might want to consider the following.

- Do you want a formal or informal garden, and what's the difference? Generally a formal garden has symmetry in its design, a balanced collection of plants and is less family-friendly by its very nature. An informal garden, on the other hand, allows you much more flexibility but can have the danger of running out of control if you try to do too much.

- Watch the progress of the sun through your garden and note the areas of greatest sun for positioning sitting areas or a greenhouse. Think about adding some shade, though, if you have babies or elderly people living with you. If you have a building or a tree in your garden, the winter sun will cast longer shadows near it, giving you a larger area of shade. Note any other areas of shade for planting shade-loving plants.

- Winds can adversely affect plants and make sitting outside unpleasant. If there's a prevailing wind in your garden, mark it with an arrow on your plan and position screens to soften the impact.

- Scale is very important. If you have a small garden, don't put a huge gazebo, summerhouse or pond in

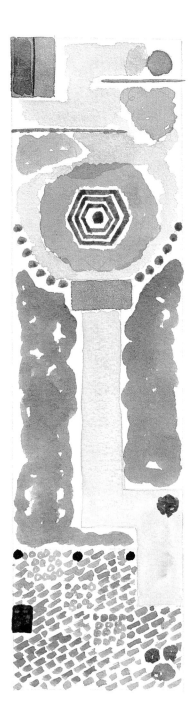

Do lots of sketches in the early stages of planning: as you experiment with ideas, you'll need to make sure the various elements are in scale with one another. See opposite for the finished look.

it as they take up an awful lot of room and will look odd. Features should look balanced, seem in proportion to each other and, what's more, 'feel' right. You can add height to your garden, even if you don't have room for that summerhouse you've always dreamed of; pergolas and rose arches with a seat under them are a good alternative.

Sloping sites don't have to be a problem. Turn them into a feature by creating terraces to give your garden an interesting, tiered effect. You can divide up the areas with walls, banks of grass or plants, or steps made from stone slabs, logs or railway sleepers.

If you live by a main road or a school where noise can drift over, put lots of planting next to the boundary fence or wall. This acts as a muffler, absorbing much of the noise. Alternatively, detract from outside noise by having running water in your garden and create an atmosphere of calm.

CONFRONT YOUR PROBLEMS

The great tendency with plans is to concentrate on the interesting new projects while everything else gets ignored. But spend time completely ignoring all the star features, and look only at those areas you don't rate too highly, such as the quirky corner adjoining the garage and the area next to the bins. Small ugly spaces they might be, but they are still part of the garden, and you can always do something with them. Either shield them from view with decorative fencing or climbers, or even consider making them into a feature by lighting them at night.

If you have one long border that doesn't amount to much, think about dividing it into two more manageable themed chunks, with an arch in the middle, leading towards a focal point. And if you don't think you have room for vegetables, try mixing them with flowers – not so that they all grow together, which sounds fun but is slightly impractical, but in well-marked, alternating beds. The shapes and colours complement each other, especially if you use ornamental forms of vegetables, such as ruby chard. The planning stage is exactly the right time to make sure the whole garden is interesting, and that it isn't all fits and starts.

A combination of strong horizontal and vertical lines draw the eye to different points in the garden, making it appear larger and more interesting. The screens at the top provide a natural look while hiding the exit.

from paper
TO REALITY

When you look at your plan, it's very hard to imagine what it will be like in reality. So the next stage is to transfer your ideas from paper back to the garden. There's always something that doesn't quite work, always something to improve on.

CHECKING THE PROPORTIONS

Use string, pegs and three-dimensional objects such as boxes as a final check that everything works. This is the last chance to fine tune. Do not skip it.

Begin with the large areas, such as borders and patios, clearly delineating them with lengths of hosepipe, clothes line or string. On the plan it is always tempting to squeeze some features slightly closer together than is really sensible just to fit in extra ideas; now you'll find out if it actually works.

Walk round the garden with a wheelbarrow, or two abreast. Are the paths wide enough? Use chairs and tables to represent different features. Can you see them from where you intended? One famously wealthy landowner in the 1930s got her staff to cut out cardboard pillars which she had them position to give the permanent site of a brand new pergola. And it worked. Without going to these extremes you can use canes, cardboard boxes and pots. And to see how many plants you might need in a certain part of a border, use balloons tied to short canes. It gives a remarkably good idea of density.

TAKING TIME

To make sure you get this stage right, leave the garden looking bizarrely surreal for a week. Keep nipping out and walking round it, trying it out, testing it, making sure it works. Can you walk round the garden in winter without sploshing through lots of mud? And is the summer seating area large enough without creating a chaos of rugs, radios and food?

The more you keep examining, the more you'll notice slight changes required. And the more of these you make, the more everything else is thrown out of kilter and the more modifications will need to be made. Compare the end result with your design plan and you'll see that there are quite a few marked changes. While you can move bedroom furniture about quite easily, shifting a whole border with all its plants 2m (6ft) to the left isn't quite as easy. First-time gardeners tend to assume they can get everything right and miss out all these checks. Those who have done it before and know the muscle-power, backache and time that go into rectifying mistakes make these checks repeatedly.

LOOKING DOWN ON THE GARDEN

While you're performing these checks, think about the views from different parts of your garden – and they will not just be along paths and across lawns. It is possible to have views across borders where low planting is suddenly used. Try to avoid a situation where the entire garden can be seen from one place. Inject mysterious corners. Gardens work best when even you, who know it best, keep finding places to explore. And the more views as you walk round a garden, the bigger even a small site will seem.

Don't forget to think about the aerial view too. Look down on the garden from a height and, using your imagination, consider the view from favoured windows. Is there something fun or beautiful to look at? Gardens do not just work from within. While a rose bed sounds like the perfect scene beneath a bedroom window, in winter it will be all bare twigs and earth. Inject features with year-round interest. Remember what they will look like after weeks of winter rain.

Laying out a hosepipe to plan the shape and size of a border is a good way of getting the right proportions. The hose can be adjusted until the border is in scale with its surroundings.

PLAN YOUR ATTACK

When you've decided exactly how your new design is going to look for real, plan the order in which you're going to work on the garden before proceeding to clear the site. Read through the relevant sections of the book to help you decide this. Generally, you should carry out all the hard landscaping – building garden structures such as paths, patios, sheds and greenhouses – before you begin planting.

The statue in this garden is used to give a focal point while the mirror behind it and the abundance of plants make the garden seem bigger than it actually is.

Some features, however, are built after planting. Plant a tree (if it's a new one) before fixing a tree seat around it (see page 45). Deciding on the order of work will also help minimize the cost of hiring equipment, so planning things carefully will pay dividends in several ways.

Disposing of heavy or bulky items, or large quantities of unwanted debris, can be made much quicker by hiring a skip.

SAVING THE GOOD PLANTS

To make good progress without damaging plants, it is important to have an open working area. Any plants that you are keeping will need protecting. Ideally, move them right out of the way where they won't get damaged; with shrubs, tie all their branches together, or wrap them round with sacking. To move a large, established shrub, see page 26. Small plants can be lifted and loosely planted (or temporarily 'heeled in') elsewhere in the garden, or be potted up and moved out of the way. Plants you don't need can be thrown away or given to neighbours.

CLEARING THE SITE

Making a mess is all part of the job, but part of the mess can actually be quite productive. It is important to work systematically when you begin clearing things up. Start by designating some areas as 'mess points' where different materials are gathered. That makes it easier to recycle and dump. For instance, all the woody plant material and prunings can be quickly fed into a hired shredder. The chippings make an excellent mulch for the borders. Dismantled hard features, such as walls and paths, should be kept separate. Part of the rubble might be suitable for

getting down
TO WORK

Spend a little time preparing the site before starting on the actual projects. You'll save yourself unnecessary hard work in the end.

MAKING IT EASY ON YOURSELF

The potential for chaos is huge. It can become quite amusing, hunting through piles of dried cement for a hammer, but it'll end up driving you barmy. Work to a system: it saves an amazing amount of time. Tools scattered over the site during the working day are easier to find if they have been clearly marked. When buying new tools, try to select those with brightly coloured handles. With existing tools, especially old favourites, a blob of brightly coloured paint on the handle can save hours of searching. To save losing tools such as hammers, chisels and screwdrivers, carry them around in a bucket.

A turf-cutting machine makes light work of lifting unwanted turf. It's only worth the hire charge, though, if you have a large area to clear.

Shredding machines are ideal for recycling woody plant material such as prunings and old (nail-free) posts. The chippings make a perfect mulch for borders, or surface for paths.

hard-core, which is used in making foundations, or for filling deep holes. Don't try feeding old timber through a shredder before checking for old nails; they ruin the blades.

WASTE NOT, WANT NOT

Topsoil, the upper 25–30cm (10–12in) of earth, is the best soil for plant growth. If you have to remove any while making new foundations, etc., make sure you keep it. Create a special area for piling up the topsoil and any turves that you have lifted. Turves can be left to break down and then dug into borders, which helps to improve the condition of the soil.

Once the site is clear, it is probably best to start constructing new features at the point furthest away from the entrance to the garden and work back towards it. This reduces the risk of damage to any work you've just done, and prevents blocking the entrance as you move materials in and out of the garden.

Saving time

If you're having deliveries of bricks and paving, etc., make sure you're in when they are delivered and have them piled up exactly where you need them. There is nothing worse than starting a job late in the day and suddenly realizing you've got to shift piles and piles of back-breaking material from the front garden to the back. It ruins tempers and wastes time.

LISTING THE EQUIPMENT

Plan the work roughly, then assess how it will actually be done to see what proportion can be done by machinery. List any tools and equipment required, and their uses, as this will help to identify which tools can be used for several tasks.

Do not spend a fortune buying special hammers and drills that you might need only once. Hiring them is best, but you must be organized about getting maximum use from them. You don't want equipment lying idle if it's on a daily hire rate. If there is going to be a huge amount of rubbish, hire a skip.

HIRING EQUIPMENT

The following is a list of tools you might need (depending on how much 'renovating' you're doing) and their uses. All the tools should be available from your local hire shop. If not, refer to the list of suppliers on page 124.

Tools for hire	Use
Rotary cultivator	Cultivation of large areas
Shredder	Chopping up organic garden waste
Turf stripper	Removing turf in strips for re-use
Spirit level	Setting and checking levels
Tape measure	Measuring and marking out
Skip	Getting rid of any rubbish, including hard materials
Claw hammer	Knocking in and removing nails
Club hammer	Knocking in pegs, breaking bricks or paving
Sledge hammer	Breaking concrete, knocking in posts
Bricklayer's trowel	Laying bricks, smoothing cement, pointing and grouting
Post-hole borer	Digging holes for posts
Shovel	Moving and mixing loose materials
Yard broom	Cleaning and tidying
Cement mixer	Mixing cement/concrete

the art of
LEVELLING

Don't be daunted by a sloping garden. There are ways to turn it to your advantage without moving tons of soil. Obviously, if you've got an extreme slope and/or you plan to be in the house for some time, it might be worth calling in the professionals.

IS FLAT BEST?

It is very easy to get obsessed by the need for a 100 per cent bump-free flat garden. But before you get ready to shift piles of earth, remember that very few garden features or structures need a totally level site; and where they do (greenhouses or gazebos, for instance), only the area for the foundation or base needs to be made level. Paths and patios actually benefit from a slight tilt because it drains the rain away. That big problem might not be so acute after all. Uneven gardens only matter when you think they do. They can still be perfectly beautiful.

LEVEL PEGGING

The easiest way to establish the level is to knock a wooden peg in the ground to the correct height, as close to the house wall as possible. This becomes the main reference level (known as the datum point); use a spirit level to take readings from this point across the garden. The best way is to use long, straight-edged wooden board, 2m (6ft) or more, and several pegs. Check the board is level before putting a peg in. Where possible, follow the natural lie of the land and modify the existing levels, perhaps trying to create a series of terraces. Radically changing the site can have adverse results, undermining nearby foundations and disrupting the natural drainage. Work within limitations

Above Digging out soil is the quickest way of adjusting levels in a garden. Fine adjustments can be made with a rake, but only if the ground has already been cultivated.

Left Logs are ideal for holding back soil, make excellent steps on a slope and are particularly fitting for a woodland setting, where natural materials are more harmonious with the surroundings.

and don't be too adventurous. The more ambitious you are, the more problems you might create. For large areas, it is possible to hire a simple optical level and a T-shaped 'boning' rod, which reduces the need for numerous pegs and marker strings all over the place. Pegs will still be used but with the rods placed on top of them to help read the correct height. This process appears complicated but is quite simple and is a much more accurate way to check levels over long distances, say 10m (30ft) or more. The main disadvantage of the system is that two people are usually required: one to take the readings and record them, the other to position the boning rods.

LETTING LEVELS DO ALL THE WORK

On sites with a gentle or undulating slope, the garden can be levelled using a technique called 'cut and fill'. The soil is scraped from the high points and used to fill the low points to achieve a reasonably level area. If the slope is steep, making cut and fill impractical, the garden can be divided into split levels or terraces. Each one is tackled individually, giving scope for a series of separate gardens.

On steeply sloping sites, long wooden pegs will be needed to take readings as you work down the slope.

Steps are far more than a means of getting from A to B. Used imaginatively, they can be an eye-catching feature in a garden and a means of displaying colourful plants.

Use a tautly tied string run from peg to peg to indicate the change in levels. This can be very helpful when gauging how much soil needs moving from the upper to the lower sections of the garden. As mentioned on page 17, if large quantities of soil are to be moved, strip off the valuable topsoil, which is the top 25–30cm (10–12in), and stack it to one side. Next, level out the subsoil and firm it, and then replace the topsoil.

Setting levels

If you are making a patio or deck attached to or positioned very close to a house or building, the level is usually determined by the position of the damp-proof course (DPC). The upper surface of the patio should be at least two layers of brick below the DPC to prevent moisture bridging across it and ruining the wall.

the
ROCK GARDEN

You can, of course, decide not to level your slope and work with Mother Nature instead. Rock gardens are an excellent way of utilizing a slope and they make terrific features. You can have them any size you want, with large or small stones. The basic structure is a mixture of rocks and free-draining soil which are cleverly arranged to imitate a natural rocky outcrop or scree. Appropriate plants inserted between the rocks give a colourful effect.

THE NATURAL LOOK

Take pictures of dramatic outcrops if you go on walking holidays to reproduce the effect on a smaller scale in your own garden. This will avoid your rock garden looking completely artificial.

If you live in an area of naturally occurring stone, you might find local stone the cheapest and the most visually pleasing. If not, go for stones with a colour that complements the look of your local surroundings. Don't be tempted to use limestone paving, though: excessive demand for natural limestone by gardeners has depleted supplies.

SITING A ROCK GARDEN

Most of the plants that thrive in rock gardens prefer plenty of sunlight and well-drained soil. Provided these two main requirements are met, rock gardens can be sited almost anywhere and are perfect for positioning on slopes. However, keep them away from overhanging trees or those that are near enough to shed leaves on them as this can cause the alpine plants to rot. Since rock gardens are big features that take some time to create (see opposite), make sure you are happy with the chosen position before committing yourself.

SIZING IT UP

A mixture of rock sizes should be used if possible, to provide a random, natural look, with several small rocks grouped around the larger ones. When choosing plants, the growth habit of each must be considered to allow enough room for natural spread and growth. Plants such as lewisias are prone to rot at soil level, so they are often planted in vertical crevices between the rocks to give them sufficient drainage.

A rock garden uses a sloping site to full advantage. Large rocks bedded into the slope provide the free drainage needed by alpine plants.

Charlie's Tips for Top Results

Place upturned pots over plants before applying a mulch to avoid getting grit, bark, or whatever on the leaves.
Any plants with hairy leaves may be damaged by wet conditions in the winter, and may need to be covered by a sheet of glass to keep off the rain.

HOW TO CREATE A ROCK GARDEN

1   When you've decided on a shape, size and style for your rockery, begin by removing the topsoil to a depth of 15cm (6in) on the site where the rock garden is to be built, and stack this to one side for later use. Fill the excavated area with coarse rubble and stones to improve the drainage, before raking soil over the rubble to form a slight mound.

2   Starting with large base rocks, move the rocks into position by dragging them or using a small excavator; they can be lifted on to the mound using crowbars or by putting a tripod over a rock and tying rope under the rock to act as a cantilever. Place the most interesting and undamaged side of each rock so that it faces outwards.

3   Position the rocks on site, tilting them slightly towards the centre of the mound. Wedge the rocks in place with stones or rubble, and pack soil behind the rocks so that the rock garden develops in layers. Fill all spaces with soil.

4   Arrange the plants (still in their pots) around the rockery to give a natural-looking effect. Using a trowel, dig a hole slightly larger than the plant's rootball. Remove the plant from its container and lower into position. Squeeze or mould the rootball to fit the plant into a crevice. Fill soil in around the rootball and firm gently. The final soil surface should just cover the compost of the rootball. When planting is completed, sprinkle a 2.5cm (1in) layer of coarse grit around the plants to form a mulch. Water the plant to settle the compost and grit.

Easy-to-grow Rock Plants
- *Allium moly*
- *Androsace jacquemontii*
- *Arabis alpina*
- *Chiastophyllum oppositifolium*
- *Gentiana acaulis*
- *Oxalis adenophylla*
- *Penstemon lyallii*
- *Phlox magellanica*
- *Saxifraga longifolia* 'Tumbling Waters'
- *Sedum spathulifolium* 'Cape Blanco'

THE SOFT TOUCH

Plants give a garden shape and colour and add year-round interest. There are hundreds and hundreds to choose from, which is part of the fun, and you don't have to be a horticulturist (or be able to pronounce all those Latin names!) to get it right.

Cobbles run into concrete drive

planting STYLE

Just as hard landscaping gives a garden a certain style and feel, so plants do the same. To help you bring out the right look for your garden, plan your planting areas in the same way you planned the other features of your garden.

PLANT ARRANGING

There are few hard and fast rules about what goes where. The best gardens often have plants in unlikely places, but they flourish none the less. The best ideas come from experimenting or by stealing ideas from other gardens. If you visit somewhere grand and come across something that you really like, make a note of what has been used where and don't be afraid to chat to the head gardener. It might save you making a costly mistake. You might even be able to buy young plants on site.

The current trend is towards gardens with a strong structure, and informal planting within. When the borders are backed by hedges, there should be a narrow path separating the two. That means that you can reach plants at the back of the border and get to the hedge when it needs trimming without having to step on plants.

Long borders can be planted as a big showpiece, as one big intricate effect, with focal points and different colours bursting through. But they are challenging. It's much easier to divide them into smaller, more manageable segments, each with a different theme, possibly divided by evergreens or short climbers growing up cane wigwams.

Island beds can be used as full stops, with big blocks of colour that end a view. Or they can be given some low plants so you can see through to the rest of the garden. Ending a garden with strong fierce colours tends to bring it forward, while soft colours make the garden seem longer. Don't forget, you can also make use of walls and fences, especially if they face south. The plants benefit from the extra heat from brickwork and direct sun, and the perfume from scented climbers will waft in through open windows.

CHECKING THE 'JIGSAW' WORKS

Work out where your planting areas are going to fall in your garden (if you haven't already done so on your plan, see page 12) and then start fine-tuning them to see if the whole thing flows. Check that the key plants and features dominate where intended, that others fit the prevailing mood, and that there are one or two surprises tucked away for discovery.

Above Broad-leaved evergreens provide a permanent framework within the garden. Planting brightly coloured flowers below them can make a shaded area seem lighter.

Left A mixed border of trees, shrubs and bedding plants is an ideal way of achieving all-year interest. Remember to keep borders in scale with the rest of the garden.

Opposite You can create a woodland setting leading down to the garden shed by making a winding path of bark mulch through a selection of shade-tolerant plants under the trees.

And at this stage, check that the plants you've chosen are right for your garden. More about this on page 29.

Check that the key plants can be seen and won't get swamped by adjacent sprawlers, and that climbers are given structures to shoot up, or nearby shrubs which they can clamber on. The big choice is making sure, when you have only limited space, that you choose plants that perform well over as long a period as possible. For example, if you have room for only three or four roses: choose ones that flower all summer rather than old-fashioned roses, such as Gallicas, which flower only once a season. The best way to choose is by visiting specialist gardens, such as the Royal National Rose Society at St Albans, Herts, or the grounds of places such as Castle Howard in Yorkshire, which have wonderful rose beds. Photographs in books and catalogues can unfairly raise expectations.

GIVING ALL-YEAR SHAPE

There might not be as much happening in a garden in the winter, but it can still look surprisingly good. Evergreens with a wide variety of hues add a huge amount of interest. Box can be topiarized in all kinds of ways, from balls and squares to pyramids. Buy a decent-sized shrub, grab a pair of secateurs, take a deep breath and shape it in the spring. Ornamental grasses can be left uncut; when covered in frost

and snow they add an extra element of interest. Even vertical structures and trellises erected mid-lawn cast shadows across the grass which punctuate the bareness.

The bones of the garden design, which really stand out over winter when the flowers are absent, can also be brought alive by repeating or contrasting key shapes. Circles and curves can be used for the borders, for insets within paths, for groupings of pots, for ponds, and for adding topiary.

PLANTING DISTANCES

Do check the eventual dimensions of plants. As a rough guide, when the plants are mature they should be just touching each other. If a plant label says a shrub spreads 1.2m (4ft) and you are planting a group of three, set them 1m (3½ft) apart. Eventually they'll form one big shape. If you want a formal garden, where you can clearly see the shape of each plant, separate them by a few extra inches.

The unavoidable problem with new gardens is that the beds will seem very sparse for the first two years, with all those gaps between plants, but they make ideal testing grounds for annuals. See which ones you prefer. They'll fill everything out *and* block out weeds. If, however, you can't bear the sight of any brown soil, you can do what Alan often does: plant much closer together, then move some of the plants later when they become crowded.

instant results
MOVING AND PRUNING

You don't have to re-do your entire garden to give it a new lease of life. Plants, shrubs and small young trees can be moved, but you never quite know how they'll react; they might go into a sulk and refuse to grow, or suddenly 'take off'. Have a go and see what happens.

HOW TO MOVE A PLANT

A plant might be large or have been growing in the same place for years, but that does not mean you cannot move it – and successfully. Provided it is moved with plenty of soil around the roots, it stands an extremely good chance of surviving and flourishing.

The first step is to dig a trench around the plant 30–60cm (1–2ft) deep. Cut through any thick, woody roots with a saw or loppers, and sever any large tap roots (usually vigorous, downward-growing roots) under the rootball. Wrap the rootball in sacking or plastic, move the plant to its new position, remove the cover, then plant immediately. Water well and mulch (see box opposite).

FLOWERS ON THE CHEAP

Check over borders of herbaceous perennials, such as anemones, catmint and phlox, that generally die back in the autumn and re-appear the following spring. If they are past their best, are too big and unmanageable, or are so good you need more, take cuttings. Use the tips of non-flowering shoots in summer. Carnations (or pinks) are

A chainsaw is ideal for removing large branches or cutting down trees, but the correct safety equipment should *always* be worn.

easily increased this way. Others, such as sedum, are increased by division. Dig them up in early spring and divide them into clumps. Re-plant the newer, vigorous outer sections and discard the tired old centre.

RENOVATING A SHRUB BY PRUNING

Many old shrubs, or those that have been badly cared for, can often be revitalized by drastic pruning. Not all shrubs respond well to this treatment. If in doubt, prune gradually over several years to see how they respond, and to avoid killing them by shock. Prune deciduous shrubs when dormant, and the evergreen kind in spring.

The follow-up programme is simple. Cut out all thin, straggly shoots and crossing branches which might rub together. Rubbing creates wounds that could lead to infection. The aim of pruning is to give a pleasing shape, and that applies equally to shrubs that are naturally lumpy things. Have a crack at imposing shape on the shapeless.

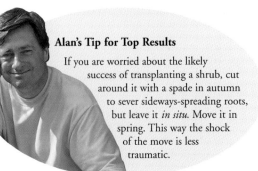

Alan's Tip for Top Results

If you are worried about the likely success of transplanting a shrub, cut around it with a spade in autumn to sever sideways-spreading roots, but leave it *in situ*. Move it in spring. This way the shock of the move is less traumatic.

HOW TO RENOVATE A SHRUB BY PRUNING

As a general rule, the best time to prune most flowering shrubs is immediately after flowering, but always check the care notes on the plant label or consult a gardening manual.

1 Prune all the weak stems to the ground. This will promote plenty of new vigorous growth from the base of the plant.

2 Cut back the main stems to within 30cm (1ft) of the base.

3 During the following winter, leave two or three of the strongest, best-placed shoots on each stump to grow, creating the new framework. Cut back the rest to the point of origin.

TREE PRUNING: REMOVING AND SHORTENING BRANCHES

Use a pruning saw to make an undercut about 30cm (1ft) away from the trunk, cutting through up to one-quarter of the branch's diameter. Then make a second cut on top of the branch, 5–7.5cm (2–3in) further along the branch. The branch will snap between these two cuts when the saw is half-way through. Finally, saw off the remaining stub close to the trunk.

If you do not cut branches this way, you will have problems. Cutting flush to the trunk from the top before some of the weight is removed will make the branch tear down into the trunk of the tree. This will create a large gaping wound, which might well become infected.

It might look easy, but pruning tree branches needs care, especially if you have not done it before. And as for using a chainsaw… Don't risk it – it's invariably best to call in a tree surgeon.

Tree Preservation Orders (TPOs)

Large, mature trees are often protected by law, even in private gardens. It is safest to assume protected status to avoid any trouble. A TPO means you must get permission from your local authority before pruning begins.

Mulching

A mulch is a thick layer of compost or leaf-mould around a plant. It feeds the soil, insulates the roots, keeps down weeds, minimizes water evaporation and is particularly important after pruning. Lay mulch at least 5cm (2in) deep to prevent water loss, and double that depth to suppress weeds.

An attractive border with well-established plants may take time to mature and a little effort to look after but is a joy to behold when it's in bloom.

preparing
BORDERS

Plants are only as good as the soil they are planted in. Before spending a fortune at the garden centre, it is vital to assess the conditions in your garden and improve them if they're not good enough. Weed and feed the soil now before you plant and the plants will get off to a racing start.

DRAINAGE

The quickest way to see if your soil is poorly drained is to dig a hole 60cm (2ft) deep and look at the colour of the soil, particularly in the lower levels. Smelly, bluish-grey soil is a sure sign of poor drainage, which causes a lack of air in the soil. The plants suffer because they develop a shallow root-system as they try to remain in the healthier topsoil. In dry summer periods, however, the topsoil dries out and the plants quickly wilt and deteriorate. Improving the drainage is essential for successful gardening and, as described below, involves adding organic matter and lots of grit.

IMPROVING SOIL

The better the soil, the healthier and more vigorous the plants. Most soils greatly benefit from the addition of organic matter just before planting, especially when dealing with permanent features such as trees and shrubs. The compost provides nutrients and fibre. It will nourish the soil in a new garden and help replace lost minerals in an older one. You can use animal manure or composted garden waste, which encourages worms, bacteria and other organisms. Avoid fresh manure, which is too strong and can damage the roots. Well-rotted manures will provide some nutrients almost immediately, and have some residual fibre. Other materials with fibre, which include composted bark, strawy manure and leafmould, are much better for improving the structure and drainage of heavy soils, and increasing moisture retention in lighter ones. These materials are ideal for long-term soil improvement because as they decompose, they contribute to the formation of humus (other decomposed matter) within the soil, which holds on to subsequent additions of nutrients.

DIGGING

When renovating an old border temporarily stripped of its plants, or creating a brand new one, digging and forking aerates and breaks up the soil deep down. Most plants prefer growing where they can root deeply; a root depth of 45–60cm (18–24in) is quite common. This depth helps them withstand drought, gives good anchorage and provides a wide source of nutrients. Dig during the autumn, before the ground becomes too wet or hard, so that the winter frosts can continue breaking up the soil.

There are two methods of digging called single and double. The names simply refer to the depth you dig; one spade, generally 25cm (10in), or two, 50cm (20in). The latter is only necessary when drainage is poor or if the ground is in bad condition.

There is no substitute for good soil preparation before planting. Trees will spend many years growing in the same soil, so thorough cultivation is a good investment for the future.

Double digging involves digging a trench 60cm (2ft) wide and two spades deep. Pile the soil into a wheelbarrow and place it for filling the last trench that you'll dig. Then stand in the first trench, use a fork to the full length of its tines to break up the bottom and work in organic matter. Next, mark out a second trench parallel to the first and use its soil to fill the first. Repeat this process across the border, filling the last trench with the soil from the first.

Additions of organic matter to the soil while you're filling the trenches are also a big boost to free-draining ground, such as chalk, improving water retention and helping plants to cope with dry conditions. Heavy, lumpy soil, such as clay, is improved because the organic matter breaks it up, making it easier to work; it also improves the drainage, oxygenates the soil and helps it warm up more quickly in the spring. For the best effect, add the organic matter evenly between the topsoil and subsoil to encourage the roots to dive down for food. When you are adding plants to a border that can't be pre-dug, give each new plant a large hole, adding plenty of organic matter.

WHAT pH IS YOUR SOIL?

It is very tempting to buy the best-looking plants you can afford but, if you stick them in the garden now, before knowing what kind of soil you've got, you might be wasting your money. Some plants need acid conditions, others alkaline. Grow most rhododendrons in alkaline soil and they'll die. You can carry out a quick and easy chemical test using an inexpensive kit from a garden centre. Most plants, such as roses, need slightly acid soil; most vegetables prefer it slightly alkaline. The alkalinity can be increased by adding lime or lime-rich matter such as mushroom compost well before planting.

Cultivated ground tends to become more acidic as lime and nutrients are washed down into the soil by rain and irrigation water, but this can be corrected by applying additional lime. Use the pH kit to make sure that additional lime is really required, as applying too much can be harmful; follow the manufacturer's instructions exactly. Avoid applying lime and manure together because the nutritional benefits of the manure are depleted by chemical reaction with lime.

Weeding
It pays to be particular and extract every last scrap of weed before planting. Weeds growing closest to plants are the hardest to eradicate, but it can be done. You might need to use a kitchen fork to prise them away. Remove every inch of the roots of perennial weeds or they can produce new plants. Annuals should be tackled before they set seed. At the very least remove the flowers as they die off.

Adding organic material to planting holes encourages new plants to root into the surrounding soil and helps them to establish rapidly.

buying and
PLANTING

Everyone thinks they know a good plant when they see one; and why not? Shopping in garden centres has become a popular pastime. But few people know what to look for. Here are some essential tips.

BARE ROOTS AND CONTAINERS

Shrubs such as roses are bought bare root or container grown. The former means they've been freshly dug from growing fields in the autumn and that their roots are free of soil, though sometimes they're packed in peat. When buying from specialist mail-order companies, this is probably what you'll get. Plant them when dormant in late autumn or early winter. Container-grown plants from garden centres can be planted at any time. In both cases avoid droughts and hard frosts.

MAKING A SELECTION

With bare-root plants always check the bark for wrinkles: they mean that the plant has dried out and will probably die. Splits or blisters might indicate rough handling or fungal diseases. Ideally, the stems and roots should be strong, with plenty of even side growth. Beware cracks, which indicate twists and breaks, the perfect places for fungal diseases to strike. Also look for shrivelling and darkening of the bark because diseases have colonized the plant and destroyed the live tissue. Container-grown plants need similar inspection. Don't be afraid to slide the plant out of the pot and look at the roots (you want pale, healthy growth), but do make sure you replace the plant carefully back in the pot.

SPOT CHECK

When you've bought all the plants you need, don't plant them straight away. Set them out in their pots. That way you'll realize you don't want a spiky-stemmed berberis next to a path, and that the exquisitely patterned tiny violas will be hidden by a 2m (6ft) high rose. Setting out the pots is the only way of getting the arrangement right.

PLANTING BARE-ROOTS

The planting procedure is similar to that for containers (see opposite) but with a few exceptions. Soak the plant's roots in a bucket of water before planting. Dig a hole at least twice the width of the plant's root system and deep

Check the roots of container-grown plants before purchase to make sure that the plants are growing well. They should have lots of new roots but not be 'pot bound'.

enough to take the roots. Break up the soil at the bottom of the hole and, after adding well-rotted manure, place the plant in the hole. Check that the soil mark on the stem is level with the surrounding surface. Replace the soil, firming as you go, shake the stem to remove any air pockets, and water round the base of the plant.

HOW TO PLANT A CONTAINER-GROWN PLANT

1 Water the container thoroughly before planting. Dig a hole at least twice the width of the plant's root system and deep enough to accommodate it all.

2 Use a garden fork to break up the bottom of the hole to help the new roots tunnel down. Apply a layer of well-rotted manure.

3 Place the plant in the centre of the hole and use a bamboo cane to check that the compost surface is 2.5cm (1in) lower than the surrounding ground.

4 Start to back-fill the hole with soil, spreading it evenly around the roots and firming as you go. Shake the stem to settle the soil. This will also remove any air pockets.

5 Apply a topdressing of fertilizer/well-rotted manure to the soil around the plant, forking it into the top 5cm (2in). This will get washed down to the roots. Water immediately round the base of the plant.

Planting depths
A bare-root rose should be planted with the bulge at the base of its stems (called the bud union) 2.5cm (1in) above ground level. All clematis should be planted with the soil surface 6cm (2½in) above where new buds form, ready to grow if the topgrowth is damaged or clematis wilt strikes.

right plant, RIGHT PLACE

The choice of plants is endless, so here is a selection of *Ground Force* favourites. All are readily available and easy to grow; simply choose ones that suit the conditions in your garden.

Cytisus battandieri has pineapple-scented flowers. Its silvery-green foliage makes it an attractive plant even when not in flower.

SHRUBS FOR STRUCTURE

These are the most important plants in a garden because they add structure and provide a good framework.

Abelia schumannii A deciduous shrub up to 1.5m (5ft) high, with arching branches bearing bronze foliage when young and green when mature; produces pink-and-white flowers that are blotched yellow on the inside from mid-summer until mid-autumn.

Berberis x ottawensis 'Superba' A vigorous shrub with arching branches up to 2.4m (8ft) long with deep reddish-purple leaves, small yellow flowers in late spring and red fruits in autumn.

Cotinus coggygria 'Royal Purple' A deciduous shrub 5m (15ft) high, with deep purple leaves and large plumes of deep pink flowers in summer.

Cytisus battandieri A semi-evergreen shrub with grey-green leaves and an open habit reaching 6m (20ft); clusters of yellow, pineapple-scented flowers in summer.

Deutzia scabra A deciduous, upright shrub reaching 3m (10ft), with dark green, oval leaves and upright clusters of white flowers in mid-summer.

Garrya elliptica An evergreen shrub with tough, dark green leaves with a wavy edge and long grey-green catkins produced from late winter; up to 3m (10ft) high.

Juniperus scopulorum 'Skyrocket' A narrow, erect conifer with silver-blue foliage, reaches up to 8m (25ft) but is only 75cm (2½ft) wide.

Lavandula angustifolia 'Hidcote' An evergreen, bushy shrub with silvery-grey foliage and dense spikes of deep purple flowers produced from mid-summer; reaches up to 1.2m (4ft) high.

Mahonia lomariifolia An erect shrub reaching 3m (10ft), with tough, narrow, evergreen foliage and spikes of fragrant, yellow flowers produced through the autumn and winter.

Viburnum tinus A compact, bushy evergreen shrub, up to 2.5m (8ft), with flattened heads of white, star-shaped flowers produced in winter and spring.

ALL-YEAR COLOUR

The following plants will make colourful additions to any garden.

Cortaderia selloana 'Sunningdale Silver' An evergreen, clump-forming pampas grass with long narrow leaves, long silvery plumes of flowers carried on stems up to 2.1m (7ft) tall in summer and lasting through the winter.

Hedera canariensis 'Gloire de Marengo' A vigorous evergreen, self-clinging climber up to 6m (20ft), leaves are deep, glossy and green, with variegated silver.

Ilex aquifolium 'Handsworth New Silver' A dense, columnar shrub up to 8m (25ft) high that has dark green leaves with a silver margin and bright red fruits in autumn and winter.

Malus sargentii A large spreading shrub up to 5m (15ft) tall with white flowers in late spring, deep red, cherry-like fruits through the autumn and winter and golden leaves in autumn.

Prunus maackii A spreading tree up to 11m (35ft) high with orange peeling bark, small white flowers in spring and butter-yellow leaves in autumn.

Pyracantha 'Mohave' A vigorous evergreen, bushy shrub reaching 4m (12ft) with oval, dark green leaves, produces small, white flowers in late spring, and orange-red fruits through the autumn and winter.

Rosa rugosa A fast-growing shrub up to 1.5m (5ft) tall, tough, leathery leaves turning gold in autumn, deep pink or white flowers in summer and large orange hips all winter.

SHADE PLANTS

While there's little you can do to make a shady garden sunny, you can work with your garden by choosing beautiful shade-loving plants.

Aquilegia vulgaris A leafy perennial with grey-green leaves and bonnet-shaped flowers in shades of white, blue, pink and red, produced on thin stems 75cm (2½ft) high.

Aquilegia vulgaris 'Nora Barlow' has unusual and attractive flowers, which are ideal for providing a bright splash in a shady garden.

Aucuba japonica 'Crotonifolia' An evergreen bushy shrub up to 2m (6ft) tall, with glossy green leaves, mottled yellow, and minute, purple flowers in mid-spring.

Cyclamen hederifolium A low-growing plant less than 15cm (6in) tall with deep green leaves, mottled silver, and pink flowers with a darker ring in the centre produced in the autumn.

Digitalis grandiflora A hardy biennial foxglove, reaching 75cm (2½ft) in height; creamy yellow tubular flowers are produced on tall spikes in summer.

Hypericum calycinum A low shrub reaching 60cm (2ft), with large, open yellow flowers throughout the summer and glossy evergreen foliage.

Mahonia aquifolium An open shrub with bright, glossy evergreen leaves which turn red in winter; small yellow flowers produced in bunches during spring.

Sarcococca humilis A low, clump-forming evergreen shrub 75cm (2½ft) high with tiny fragrant white flowers in late winter.

Tiarella cordifolia A vigorous ground-cover plant with pale green leaves tinged bronze in winter; spikes of small white flowers in spring and summer.

DROUGHT-TOLERANT PLANTS

Although the following plants can withstand dry conditions, you can still conserve water by adding a thick layer of mulch.

Allium christophii An ornamental onion with globes of metallic pink, star-shaped flowers held on stout 60cm (2ft) stems in summer.

Calendula officinalis The 'pot marigold', has miniature orange 'chrysanthemum' flowers held above the mid-green leaves on 60cm (2ft) stems throughout the summer.

Gleditsia triacanthos 'Sunburst' A small, deep-rooted tree with light, delicate foliage, reaching 9m (30ft) and flowering in mid-summer.

Nerine bowdenii Elegant, pink lily-like blooms in late summer carried on slender, green stems up to 45cm (18in) high above arching green leaves.

Osteospermum 'Whirligig' Showy, daisy-like flowers with white spoon-tipped petals and a blue reverse, glossy mid-green foliage, up to 75cm (2½ft) tall.

Phormium tenax A clump-forming, evergreen perennial, with strap-like leaves and orange flowers held on 1.5m (5ft) stems in summer.

Sedum spectabile Wide, flat heads with small, star-like, pink or white flowers in late summer on 60cm (2ft) high stems, and thick, fleshy grey-green leaves.

Verbascum chaixii A tall spike of sulphur-yellow flowers in summer up to 1.5m (5ft) high, emerging from a rosette of silver-haired leaves.

Yucca filamentosa Strap-like leaves ending in a sharp spine, with a tall spike of up to 1–1.2m (3–4ft) carrying white, bell-shaped flowers.

Planting in groups of three or five establishes plant communities and helps give the impression of maturity in a new garden.

...and more
RIGHT PLANTS

Here are lots more plants for other conditions that may exist in your garden.

LOW-MAINTENANCE PLANTS

If you're a busy person with little time to look after your garden, choose more permanent planting and fewer annuals to cut down your workload in spring.

Agapanthus campanulatus An evergreen perennial with long, strap-like, green leaves and large globes of small, blue or white, lily-like flowers held on green stems 1m (3ft) above the ground; flowers mid- to late summer.

Camellia x williamsii **'Donation'** An acid-loving, evergreen shrub up to 3m (10ft) high; glossy leaves and cup-shaped pink flowers with several rounds of petals in spring.

Choisya ternata An evergreen shrub with a rounded shape reaching 2.5m (8ft), dense, glossy green, aromatic foliage with clusters of fragrant white flowers in the spring.

Hamamelis mollis **'Pallida'** A large deciduous shrub with erect growth up to 3m (10ft) high, producing spidery, sulphur-yellow flowers on bare stems in early spring; leaves turn golden yellow in the autumn.

Magnolia stellata A dense, bushy shrub or small tree up to 3m (10ft) high, producing pure white, star-shaped flowers on bare stems in early spring.

Pleioblastus viridistriatus An evergreen, slow-spreading bamboo up to 1.25m (4ft) with yellow leaves striped green.

Rosa glauca A vigorous rose up to 2.5m (8ft) tall with attractive, grey-purple leaves and small, five-petalled flowers coloured cerise-pink with a yellow centre in early summer.

WIND-RESISTANT PLANTS

Choose sturdier plants where wind is a problem and protect them by placing screens to act as a windbreak.

Calluna vulgaris Low-growing, mat-forming heather with white, pink or red flowers in late summer; prefers lime-free soil.

Crataegus laevigata **'Paul's Scarlet'** A small tree of 8m (25ft) in height with double red flowers in early summer and good autumn leaf colour.

Plants can be used to link different elements within a garden. Gravel, large cobbles and wooden posts, for example, can be softened and enhanced by suitable planting.

Escallonia 'Apple Blossom' Colourful evergreen with glossy green leaves and white flowers flushed pink, up to 2.4m (8ft) high.

Festuca glauca A dwarf, evergreen grass with tufts of grey-blue foliage and flower stalks up to 45cm (18in) tall in summer.

Rhododendron yakushimanum This dome-shaped plant will gradually reach 1.2m (4ft) high; the pink flowers are produced in late spring and the new foliage has a thick, white felt covering.

Sinoarundinaria nitida A rapidly growing, green bamboo shoots up to 4m (12ft) tall and produces dull, grey-green leaves the following spring and summer.

Tamarix ramosissima A small tree of 5m (15ft) high with slender, arching stems carrying narrow green foliage and pink flowers in late summer.

EASY-CARE PERENNIALS FOR SUN OR PART SHADE

Perfect for the low-maintenance gardener, these plants pretty much look after themselves.

Acanthus spinosus Bold spikes of mauve-purple flowers carried on stems up to 1.5m (5ft) high with attractive, deeply cut leaves; this plant can be positioned in either sun or part shade.

Campanula lactiflora Showers of bell-shaped pink, blue or white flowers throughout the summer on stems up to 1.5m (5ft) high; suitable for part shade.

Dicentra spectabilis 'Bleeding heart' is one of the very best perennials, with heart-shaped, pinky-red flowers with a white tip; reaches up to 1m (3ft) and should be planted in part shade.

Euphorbia griffithii 'Fireglow' A green, leafy, bushy plant which has deep-orange flower heads in early summer on stems up to 1.2m (4ft) tall; suitable for part shade.

The vibrantly coloured nasturtium *Tropaeolum majus* 'Alaska Mixed' is a perfect choice for a border where 'hot' colours are part of the colour scheme.

Acanthus spinosus, with its spine-clad flower stems, is capable of taking care of itself, and will grow almost anywhere.

Hemerocallis hybrids – 'Daylilies' are hardy, adaptable and available in a wide range of flower colours on stalks 1m (3ft) tall; sun or dappled shade.

Iris germanica The 'bearded iris' has three-pronged flowers in a wide range of colours, up to 1.2m (4ft); likes sun.

Schizostylis coccinea Arching grass-like leaves and erect spikes of pink or red, lily-shaped flowers up to 60cm (2ft) tall; position in sun.

NO-NONSENSE ANNUALS

A simple way to provide instant colour. There are literally hundreds of annuals on the market; choose ones that will complement your colour scheme.

Alyssum maritimum Low-growing plants of 15cm (6in) or under trail along the ground and produce white, pink or purple flowers in summer.

Centaurea cyanus The 'cornflower' has single or double flowers in shades of red, white, blue and pink, held above the foliage on stems 90cm (3ft) tall.

Eschscholtzia caespitosa Poppy-like flowers in shades from cool white to hot orange borne on slender, waving stems up to 45cm (18in) tall.

Iberis umbellata 'Candytuft' has white, pink or purple flowers opening from the centre outwards on 20cm (8in) stems in summer.

Nigella damascena Up to 60cm (2ft) tall stems carry circular flowers ranging from white to rose pink and blue in summer.

Papaver rhoeas The poppy has large, green buds carried on slender, 60cm (2ft) green stems; summer flowers in shades of red, white and pink.

Phlox drummondii Semi-circular heads of small, star-like flowers produced on 20cm (8in) stems above narrow, mid-green leaves.

Tropaeolum majus – Small, trumpet-shaped flowers ranging from cream through to yellow and orange to deep red; spreading growth is up to 30cm (12in) high.

STRUCTURED GARDENING

Gardening isn't just about flowers. It's about adding all kinds of fun extras, from tree seats to ornamental paths to colourful decking. 'Hard landscaping' adds style and year-round interest, as well as giving the plants an extra framework.

which hard SURFACE?

Paving is paving, isn't it? Well, no, it isn't – but do we actually take much notice of it as we walk from A to B? Hard surfaces, such as pathways and patios, are often taken for granted, but choosing one that suits the surroundings and the planting scheme will make a big difference to the finished garden. Have a good look around at the different surfaces available – from paving slabs, paviors and bricks to cobbles and setts (stone cubes or blocks) – before you decide.

SELECTING HARD SURFACES FOR SPECIFIC USES

Hard surfaces should not dominate the garden, but act as background and a framework for the plants. The use of the hard surface is a major consideration, and the type of 'traffic' that is expected over a particular area will help determine the kind of materials used and the nature and depth of any foundations. For most garden paths and patios that means light usage for light equipment such as lawn-mowers and wheelbarrows.

COLOURS AND TEXTURES

Different coloured surfaces provide a variety of effects. Light colours help increase light levels in shady areas, coloured flooring can complement or contrast with nearby plantings, and a material similar to the walls of the house will visually link the garden and the building.

Whichever surface you choose, lay it with a gentle fall or slope to let the rain run away in a certain direction. The only problem occurs when the slope is barely perceptible and the conditions are wet or icy: it gets dangerous. The problem is increased if the surface has been given a smooth finish. Using a roughly textured or slightly ridged surface provides style and interest while improving safety, particularly for children and the elderly. Don't make it too coarse, though; this type of textured surface should be comfortable enough to walk on in bare feet.

PATTERNS

There are ingenious ways of fooling the eye and visually suggesting the garden has a slightly different shape. For example, a linear pattern running down the garden

Left Using materials with different surfaces and textures can create pleasing contrasts in a garden. But, as shown here, a sense of unity can be achieved by introducing objects made of the same materials.

Above Patterns made with bricks and slabs can be used to create a sense of flow and movement through a garden, while different colours may be used to define one section before moving on to the next.

Above Arranging slabs in a slightly staggered fashion will make a path appear to meander and give the impression that a view or walk is longer than it actually is.

Right Special features can be incorporated into a pattern of bricks or slabs as it is laid. Here a child's sandpit is central to the design, but does not dominate.

creates the illusion of length, while paving running across the area will create a sense of width. Patterns such as basket weave provide no definite direction, and can be used in those areas where you wish to stop and look, or sit and rest. On the other hand, stretcher bond (where most of the bricks run in one direction) will hurry the observer into another part of the garden. Patterns can be used to give the hard surface 'pace' to influence our movement in the garden.

BUDGET

Building a path or patio can be expensive, especially if you're not re-using bricks or slabs from an old patio, so make sure you have a budget to cover the whole job. If you're using different-sized slabs to create a random pattern, work it out on paper first but order equal areas of each size, not equal numbers, or you'll end up with too many larger slabs.

Which style?
The most important tip is to keep patterns clear and simple. The secret of good design is to avoid mixing too many different materials, as they create a busy, distracting effect. It is possible, though, to begin a path in one style, then, after 6m (20ft), develop another, and so on. This adds interest, especially to the winter garden.

firm foundations for
PATHS AND PATIOS

Any paved area that must provide support or carry any form of load must have a firm base to reduce the chance of subsidence or collapse. Foundations provide the main substance and strength, while the surface layer provides some support and all the decorative finish.

FOUNDATIONS

At their simplest, foundations can be sand over compacted soil. This is perfectly adequate for heavy materials such as railway sleepers and big slabs because they have a large surface area and are therefore very stable. In the case of smaller paving units, such as cobbles or setts (stone cubes or blocks), a prepared foundation of compacted rubble covered with sand and compacted again to give a level base is needed to reduce movement after they have been laid. Deeper foundations for heavy outbuildings, such as brick sheds and garages, consist of a sub-base and a base: the sub-base is made of compacted sand and gravel (or builder's rubble), and the base layer is concrete or compacted sand (see step 3, opposite).

In order to make a firm, level foundation, a wooden or metal frame, known as shuttering or form-work, is made and supported by several pegs, say, one every 1m (3½ft), inserted into the soil. This frame is usually slightly larger than required, and must be checked for levels and the accuracy of all right angles before any concrete is poured into it. The more complicated the shape of the foundation, the greater the amount of shuttering required.

To make concrete you need 1 part cement, 2 parts sand and 4 parts coarse aggregate. For laying paving on top of concrete (when dry), use a mortar mix. This is made up of 4 parts sharp sand, 2 parts soft sand and 1 part cement. Add water and plasticizer (which keeps the mixture pliable for longer) at about 50ml (2 fl oz) to every 50kg (110lb) of cement.

FLEXIBLE PAVING

Any surface that has bricks and paviors not cemented in place but laid on sand is referred to as flexible paving. This is because the tiny gap between each brick, which is infilled with sand, allows them to move slightly as traffic passes over. Flexible paving is used for paths, walks and driveways and has increased in popularity because it is easier to lay, can be lifted and re-laid, and is much easier to repair.

PAVING – COVERAGE RATES

One tonne will cover approximately…

Material	Area in sq m (sq yd)
Cobbles 5 x 7.5cm (2 x 3in)	6.5–7.0 (7.7–8.3)
Gravel 2.5cm (1in) deep (loose)	30 (35.8)
Gravel 5cm (2in) deep (rolled)	12 (14.3)
Setts 10 x 10 x 10cm (4in)	3.7–4.0 (4.4–4.7)
Bedding sand 5cm (2in) deep; 1 cu m (35.3 cu ft)	24–25 (28.7–29.9)
Sharp sand 5cm (2in) deep; 1 cu m (35.3 cu ft)	19–20 (22.7–23.9)
Bricks (laid flat)	36 (43.0)
Bricks (laid on edge)	54 (64.6)
Paviors	39–49 (46.6–58.6)
Slabs 60 x 60cm (2ft)	2.75 (3.2)

After slabs have been laid, brushing in a mixture of sand and cement helps to weatherproof the joints.

LAYING FLEXIBLE BRICK PAVING

1   Mark out the shape of the paved area using a string line and wooden pegs. Strip away the surface debris in the marked area, and dig out the soil to a depth of about 15cm (6in), the correct depth for paths which are being used only for light traffic.

2   Compact the base with a post or heavy rake, but for large areas a plate vibrator can be hired.

3   The margins of the paved area are made from bricks laid on their edge in a stacking bond, bedded on to a damp mortar mix, checked with a spirit level to keep the surface level. When the edging course of bricks has set, the inner sections of the area are covered with a layer of dry sand 7–8cm (3–3 1/2 in) deep, spread until it is level and compacted using a board or plank with a straight edge.

4   Bed the bricks on to the sand, leaving a gap of 2mm (a matchstick width apart) between each, and when an area is finished, brush over with dry sand to fill the spaces between the bricks.

5   Finally, compact the bricks into the sand using a plate vibrator or a board and mallet. If using a plate vibrator, tie a piece of old carpet on to it to prevent the surface of the bricks from being scratched.

Tommy's Tip for Top Results

With patios, decks and foundations it is vital that the square or rectangular base is made up of right angles, at least where intended. Use a builder's square to check. It's costly to remedy mistakes if you don't get it right.

BUILDING WALLS
in gardens

Walls are separated into two kinds: dividing (or ornamental) and retaining ones. The latter are used to support soil where a garden is on split levels, or where the neighbouring garden is higher or lower. Retaining walls may also be used to create raised beds, which are easier for disabled or elderly gardeners when bending is a problem.

WALLING MATERIALS

There are many different materials suitable for garden situations. Depending on the effect required, a wall can be of brick, dry stone, concrete blocks or timber. Stone, brick and concrete last for many years, but wooden walls will have an effective life of about 25 years only, especially where the timber is in contact with the soil. Obviously, your choice will depend on how long you're intending to stay in your home and your budget.

LOAD-BEARING WALLS

Any walls that must support an overhead weight (e.g. cross-beams on pergolas, roof supports, plant supports) must

have square supports, called piers, incorporated at regular intervals to provide support and strength. These piers must be at least twice the thickness of the wall to provide sufficient structural support. A single-thickness brick wall that is going to be higher than 45cm (18in) or a double-thickness brick wall higher than 1.25m (4ft) will need to have piers every 3m (10ft). Retaining walls often have gaps ('weep holes') between the bricks to allow the soil to drain and to reduce the weight behind the wall. To cope with the weight of soil being retained, a wider and deeper foundation is often used.

RAILWAY SLEEPERS

These are an excellent, simple alternative to brick-built retaining walls and are usually cheaper. You'll find them at yards specializing in recycled or demolition materials and, as they are heavily impregnated with wood preservative, they last a very long time. Ordinary nails will keep them together as their weight ensures that they stay in place. In hot weather, railway sleepers occasionally ooze wood preservative. This can be soaked up by sprinkling dry sand on to wet patches.

Left Where a wall is planned, it is helpful to arrange some of the bricks or blocks without mortar in order to get some idea of what the finished wall will look like.

Opposite A retaining wall must have enough strength to hold back large volumes of soil. Always bear in mind that the soil and plants it retains can become much weightier when they have been soaked by heavy rain.

How many bricks?
- 1 cu m (33 cu ft) of mortar will be sufficient to lay approximately 2,600 bricks.
- About 54 bricks are needed to lay 1 sq m (1.2 sq yd) of wall of half-brick thickness.
- About 108 bricks are needed to lay 1 sq m (1.2 sq yd) of wall of a full brick's thickness.

BUILDING A RETAINING WALL WITH RAILWAY SLEEPERS

1   Mark out the area and dimensions of the raised bed, and remove any surface vegetation from within the marked area.

2   Lay out the sleepers to create a low wooden wall for the planting bed. On the bottom layer of sleepers, leave a 2.5cm (1in) open gap between the end of each sleeper to allow surplus water to drain away.

3   Repeat the process, working around the wall, stacking sleepers to the required height. Drive 15cm (6in) nails into the corner joints at an angle on every other row of sleepers to keep them stable.

4   When the wall has reached the required height, fix the top row by driving 15cm (6in) nails at an angle through the vertical joints.

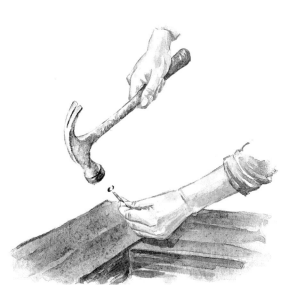

DECKING

Wood is an excellent flooring material for the garden. It has a warm, natural feel which cannot be matched by any other material, and good-quality wood can last for many years depending on the type – hard or soft, how long it has been seasoned, how well it is treated, the material used as a preservative, and whether the wood is in contact with the soil.

DECKING AREAS

If it's a sunny enough spot to be a pleasant seating place, the most obvious area to deck is that adjoining the house because it's handily situated for carrying trays, etc. in and out. But you can of course put decking anywhere you like in the garden. You can have a low-level deck (see opposite page) that sits almost on the ground or a raised deck (see page 46) like a veranda, a decked path or a play area fitted with a gate if you have toddlers. The size of the deck should allow plenty of room round tables and chairs and should be wide enough for through traffic to move easily between house and garden.

CHOOSING THE WOOD

Wood rot is the number one enemy, especially with decks on or close to the soil. If an unsuitable type of timber is chosen, the deck will last only about five years. Softwood is the most commonly used material but it must be pressure treated or vacuum impregnated to ensure that the preservative penetrates deep into the wood. Alternatively, decay-resistant wood can be used from some trees, including teak, western red cedar and oak, especially if the oak is green (unseasoned). Such wood can be very expensive, even if it is recycled, but it will last for many years. For outdoor use, decking boards should be at least 2.5–5cm (1–2in) thick to prevent the wood twisting or warping from the constantly fluctuating moisture levels as the wood regularly dries and gets wet from the changing weather. Ideally, treat the wood with a clear or coloured preservative or paint it every two to three years. The new water-porous paints are an ideal way of changing a colour scheme quickly and relatively cheaply. Note that wet timber can be slippery, but if given a slightly roughened finish should be safe.

Decking is a popular way of making attractive paths and seating areas. The wood has a warm, welcoming appearance and is pleasing to touch.

existing hard surface because the main burden of supporting the deck is transferred to the surface rather than the joists.

The deck is levelled by placing thin slivers or wedges of wood, called 'shims', between the supporting joists and the concrete below. This is a technique which is often used on the floor of a roof garden, where it is important to spread the weight evenly in order to prevent damage to the roof itself.

SIZE OF BOARDS

Narrow decking boards can also be used to create the illusion that an area is larger than it really is, while fewer, broader boards can make an area appear smaller. If boards of mixed widths are used, it is important to keep regular gaps between them to ensure uniformity. The direction the boards are laid will also influence the impression of space. A diagonal pattern or one where the boards run away from the viewer will feel more spacious than one where the boards are laid side to side.

INSTANT FOUNDATIONS

The most common and usually the easiest type of deck to build is low-level decking. As long as the ground is roughly level, little digging and foundation work is required. Low-level decks are perfect for covering an old concrete or paved patio, which can be used to form the foundation of the new deck. Smaller, cheaper joists can be used on an

Getting the most out of trees

Other areas of the garden lend themselves to the use of wooden decks and seating, particularly around the base of a tree. The advantage is that no foundations are required which immediately reduces the risk of damaging the tree and its roots. On the contrary, the decking can be a means of protecting them.

types of
DECKING

The veranda outside this shed is a good example of how to create a level sitting area on a sloping site. The hand rail is both a decorative and a safety feature.

Decking not only looks attractive but can cover a multitude of sins. Decks are often laid on roughly levelled ground where little digging and foundation work is required.

RAISED DECKS

Decks raised 60cm (2ft) or more above ground level can be more difficult to construct than low-level decks. You might need to consult a structural engineer to calculate load-bearing requirements and dimensions for the deck, particularly from a health and safety point of view. Once these figures have been determined and the appropriate wood selected, much of the construction is similar to that of low-level decks (see pages 48 and 49), although well-planned and constructed foundations are essential.

Equally important is a safety hand rail, usually 1.2m (4ft) above the deck, and vertical balusters or slats fitted between the deck surface and the hand rail to stop children falling through.

Alan's Tip for Top Results

When making a large area of deck, build several separate sections of decking and fit them together. If any valuable items, such as jewellery or money, should fall through a gap, one section can be easily lifted to retrieve the item without damaging the deck.

FITTING DECKS TO OTHER STRUCTURES

With decks that form balconies or similar structures, special care has to be taken to fit them to the adjoining building, which becomes one of the main anchor points, particularly if the deck is being built out over a slope. A wallplate, consisting of a section of stout, flat timber fastened to the wall of the building, will support the load-bearing joists which carry the decking boards. For major projects such as this you will need the hired help of your local Tommy. Also note that planning permission might be required. This will usually depend on the area of the decking surface and its height above ground, especially if it means that a neighbour's property is going to be overlooked.

FIXTURES, SEATS AND FITTINGS

Since most wooden decks are designed and built as seating areas, it is easy to incorporate seats, benches and tables into the deck as it is being built. They are usually fitted to the upright posts which support the hand rails or safety barriers. This provides comfort and convenience and adds to the strength of the decking.

Where garden furniture is built into the decking or its supports, good use can be made of dead space under the seats and tables. It can be used as cupboards or boxes for storing folding seats, awnings and cushions, and other items, including barbecue equipment and gardening tools.

Above Where seating and other types of furniture are built on a deck, the spaces beneath the seats and beneath the deck itself make ideal storage areas for gardening tools and equipment. Weatherproof such storage areas by laying plastic sheeting inside them.

Left This raised deck, with broad planks and stout upright posts, resembles a quay, fitting in with the coastal theme of the garden. As the planting becomes established, the upright posts could become supports for climbers.

all hands
ON DECK

You don't have to be a top-notch carpenter to lay decking. Take your time and double-check levels to avoid making mistakes. Tommy has only two days to build decking from scratch: you can afford to take a little longer... and achieve the same results.

SIZE OF WOOD AND SCREWING

Plan carefully and use complete sections of timber wherever possible to avoid making joints which may weaken the structure. Pre-drilling the deck boards before nailing them to the joists will help prevent the wood from splitting, especially at the ends.

For most types of wood, galvanized or zinc-plated nails or screws should be used to prevent the wood becoming rusted and stained. Where green (unseasoned) oak is used, stainless steel fixings will reduce the risk of metal corrosion and wood rot. Always nail through the thinner wood into the thicker supports and drive the nails into the wood at a slight angle to give the structure added strength. When screws are used to hold down the decking boards, their heads must be countersunk into the wood to prevent injuries to toes and feet.

FITTINGS, SUPPORTS AND FOUNDATIONS

In order to extend the useful life of the decking and create a reasonably level surface, lay the deck on a foundation that reduces or prevents any contact between the soil and wood. Use a prepared base of compacted ash or sand but, where an adjustment in levels is required, set concrete pads into the ground at regular intervals to carry supporting beams called 'stringers'. These stringers will need support themselves at set intervals to prevent the whole deck from sagging or developing an uneven surface. As a rough guide, stringers which are 100 x 50mm (4 x 2in) will need to be supported by the foundations every 1.5m (5ft) along their length. Stringers are usually positioned to run at right angles to the deck boards. Where a site is uneven, any adjustment to the level is normally made at the foundation stage.

Non-slip surfaces
To minimize the possibility of slipping, leave slight gaps between each board. This gives a better grip and helps any water quickly drain away.

Left Stepped decking, which has each section of planks running in a different direction, creates a terrific sense of space. As always with decking, the heads of nails and screws must be countersunk to avoid injury.

Right Where decking sits on a wooden framework, the supports must be secured with bolts or coach screws. These will prevent the structure from swaying and enable it to support the weight of people standing on it.

HOW TO LAY DECKING

1   Dig out the soil to the required depth and set the brick or concrete pads into the ground, checking at regular intervals to ensure that they are level using a plank and spirit level.

2   Cut the support joists to length, position them on the base pads and bolt or screw them firmly into position. Check that they are level.

3   Lay out the decking boards and drill them before nailing them into position. Start at one end, and work systematically across the deck area, leaving a space of about 1cm (¹⁄₂in) between the individual boards.

4   Cut away any surplus sections of decking, and treat the cut ends with a wood preservative. The wood that has been cut across the grain is likely to start rotting first.

LAWNS

Lawns are too easily taken for granted, but ignore them at your peril. They can quickly become tired, bald and clapped out. Keeping them in tip-top condition requires such little effort, and the results can be quite amazing. Good gardens need good lawns.

Davina

the kiss of life for
AN OLD LAWN

In this garden the lawn draws the eye to the focal point, a statue in the far border. The lawn itself provides a low contrast to the height and colours of the borders on each side.

There's nothing worse than a lawn that isn't growing well. However beautiful the rest of the garden looks, a poor lawn will spoil the picture. But don't despair – it can easily be revived by following a few simple techniques.

IMPROVING A TIRED LAWN

It is essential that you mow the lawn regularly from spring to autumn, keeping the grass and weeds down to a height of 5cm (2in) in the spring. Then rake off all the cuttings and any dead grass, called thatch. This will make the lawn look a complete mess, but it will recover within about 10 days.

Next, give the lawn a dressing of fertilizer (which includes a weed-killer) to encourage grass growth. Any remaining problems can be tackled in the autumn by applying an autumn lawn-feed (which will harden the grass growth against the winter cold). Choose a feed combined with a moss killer. The latter makes the lawn look black as the moss starts to die, but wait until the dead moss turns brown before raking it out. Do not compost this – it contains too many chemicals. Any patches of moss that survive the first treatment can be given a repeat treatment to eradicate the problem; well-established moss might take two to three attempts before it is fully controlled.

KEEPING LAWNS IN SHAPE

Lawns are most susceptible to pest and disease attack when they are in poor health. By keeping the grass healthy, you will reduce and control common pests and diseases, reducing the need to apply chemicals.

When mowing, always follow the one-third rule. That means don't cut more than one-third of the height of the grass in a single cut or you will harm the lawn. Mowing too short will stress the grass and encourage weeds to develop as sunlight reaches the soil. Stress also impedes growth, allowing moss to invade in the spring and autumn, and reduces drought-tolerance in summer.

TOPDRESSING

Adding bulky materials, such as sand, soil and peat-substitute mixtures, to help overcome certain lawn problems is known as topdressing. It can be done either on the surface to modify levels or incorporated into the lawn to improve the rooting zone. Where the topdressing is used to improve the soil, the lawn should be spiked to create lots of tiny holes into which the topdressing can be brushed. On heavy soils, such as clay, the small holes are filled with a sandy mixture to improve soil drainage, helping reduce waterlogging and standing surface water. Where the soil is light and free-draining, use a topdressing with a high proportion of soil and peat substitute to hold water and reduce drying out.

Where topdressing is used to fill hollows, this should be done gradually – no more than a 2.5cm (1in) layer at any one time – so that the grass can grow through the filling. Thicker layers of topdressing can kill the grass through lack of light.

Spiking a lawn aerates compacted soil. It allows roots to breathe, encouraging new leaf growth and a healthier lawn.

OXYGENATING

Healthy lawns need air in the soil. Spiking the lawn and brushing compost or sand into the spike holes must be done before any bare patches of lawn are re-seeded or turfed. Also make sure that the soil is not compacted because this starves the roots of oxygen, making the grass thin, yellow and patchy.

Worms are good news

Don't be alarmed by casts. They might not look good, but worms are excellent at improving drainage and devouring dead grass. Simply brush off dry casts before mowing.

BARE PATCHES

Areas where little or no grass grows can easily be rectified. The best time to do this is in May or September after it has rained but when the lawn is dry. Lightly fork over the patch and remove any weeds. Rake the area level, sow the seed and rake again. Do not water until the seeds germinate.

WATERING YOUR LAWN

Lawns need regular watering during dry spells to keep them looking healthy and luscious; sprinklers are ideal for this (as long as there isn't a hose-pipe ban). A short sprinkle, however, will only dampen the surface, bringing the grass roots to the top and making them vulnerable to drying out. Water long enough to wet the soil.

MAKING a lawn

If a lawn is totally beyond repair, it's sometimes easier to make a new one. On *Ground Force* we use turf because it gives instant results. However, it's much cheaper using seed, if you can be patient, and you can buy a mix specially geared to your needs.

OUT WITH THE OLD

The first thing you need to do is to remove the old turf. This can be done in two ways: manually with a spade, or with a turf stripper, as used by the team on *Ground Force*. (Turf strippers are relatively new on the market but your local hire shop might stock them.) Or you can kill the old turf by spraying the grass with a weedkiller (glyphosate) and digging it up when the grass is dead, which will take 6–8 weeks. Peel off the turf with a spade and stack it (turves upside-down) to form compost. The best times to create a new lawn are early autumn or mid-spring.

PREPARING THE SITE

As with most things, preparation is the key to success: the cleaner the soil from weeds, stones and debris, the fewer the problems. When you've got rid of your old turf, begin by digging the soil to the full depth of a garden fork's tines, removing all weeds, roots and rubble. When this is done, levelling can begin. Tackle the area with a large-toothed rake to level it roughly. Break up large clods and smooth out undulations, leaving a coarse-textured finish. Then firm the soil by walking across the area, applying pressure with the heels of your boots. Rake a second time using a fine-toothed rake, breaking up the soil and creating a fine-textured finish. Remove any remaining large stones and pieces of debris, such as bits of root, and rake level to remove all your footprints. Finally, walk the area again, then give the soil a final raking (a base dressing of fertilizer can be added at this stage, if required). The area is now ready for seed sowing or turfing.

SELECTING THE RIGHT TYPE OF GRASS SEED

Some garden centres and all specialist feed suppliers have types of different seeds. You can have any mix you want, depending on your needs. Fine grasses suit an ornamental

Left A well-manicured lawn is often the centrepiece of a perfect garden. There's no doubt that a fresh, green turf, mown into stripes, is a very satisfying sight.

Right When the seedlings reach this stage, three weeks after germination, the lawn should be lightly rolled to encourage grass plants to produce new shoots from soil level.

Raking the soil helps to remove stones and debris. It is also the best way of making a level surface and a firm seedbed before sowing grass seed.

GERMINATION

Grass seed will usually germinate within 10–14 days. You might need to water the area if the soil becomes very dry and the seeds are not germinating. Three weeks after germination the grass should be rolled lightly to encourage tillering, that is, the production of shoots from the base. The greater the number of new leaves and shoots, the thicker the lawn will become.

BIRD PROTECTERS

If you see birds pecking at the grass seed, don't be too concerned as the seed usually contains a repellent which makes them spit it out again almost immediately.

WHAT GOES WHERE?

Below is a list of the combination and proportion of seeds you'll need to grow the lawn of your choice.

lawn, tougher hard-wearing grasses are best for a children's play area, and a shade-tolerant grass is required under trees.

SOWING AND GROWING

Choose a dry, still day when the soil is slightly moist, and mark part of the lawn into areas of 1 sq m (1 sq yd). Sow each square with approximately 30–45g (1–1½oz) of seed, giving good even coverage by sowing half the seed across the plot, and the remainder at right angles. Then rake the seed lightly into the surface.

Seed mixtures		Purpose
Browntop bent	20%	Fine lawns
Chewings fescue	30%	
Creeping red fescue	50%	
Browntop bent	10%	Hard-wearing lawns
Chewings fescue	40%	
Creeping red fescue	20%	
Perennial rye grass (dwarf cultivars)	30%	
Browntop bent	10%	Dry soil lawns
Creeping red fescue	20%	
Hard fescue	30%	
Slender red fescue	30%	
Smooth-stalked meadow grass	10%	
Browntop bent	10%	Lightly shaded lawns
Chewings fescue	30%	
Creeping red fescue	35%	
Smooth-stalked meadow grass	25%	

CARPET-LAYING
for gardeners

Laying turf is a bit like laying carpet. In fact, turf was once used on the roofs of houses as insulation. In its more conventional setting it provides a quick covering, easily knits into place and is the ultimate in transforming a garden instantly.

A LIVING CARPET

Although turf is seen as a quick-fix instant lawn, it actually involves as much preparation as seed to ensure it has a good base on which to grow. Do all the preparation work before the turf is delivered. You can leave the turf stacked for about three days, after which the outside of the rolls will dry and crack, and the grass inside will turn to compost from the heat and moisture and lack of light. If it's not possible to lay the turf in this time, open the rolls and lay them out loosely so that the living grass is exposed to the light. This prevents rapid deterioration of the turf before it is laid. If the weather is warm and dry, water the grass at least once a day. If possible, avoid buying turf grown on soil that incorporates a plastic mesh. The mesh is for the convenience of suppliers, but it's a terrible nuisance to gardeners, catching in the tines of forks and posing a hazard to the blades of mowers.

LAYING AND CARING FOR TURF

Begin by preparing the site as for seed-sowing (see page 54), then mark out the lawn edge using a wooden plank or garden line. Lay the turves along at least two edges of the lawn area, working out from a corner, if possible, across the plot. Open each roll of turf, pressing it firmly into place against the preceding one. Push the turves together to close any gaps or joints, but arrange them in a brickwork pattern.

Always work in a forward direction to prevent walking on prepared soil, standing on a plank on the turf that has been laid. This firms the turf into position and prevents damage by footprints as the next row of turves is laid. Where there is an overlap at the end of a row, make the fit by laying one piece edging over the other and trim the lower one to size. Remove any surplus so that the top piece of turf fits snugly. Finally, when all the turf has been laid, sweep it with a stiff brush to lift the flattened grass and remove any stones and soil. Water the area thoroughly with a sprinkler so that the soil beneath the turves is wet.

Mowing can start about 10–14 days after the turf has been laid. Set the blades to a height of 5cm (2in) to check the growth slightly and encourage rooting into the soil.

REPAIRING THE LAWN

If humps or hollows develop due to localized settlement in the lawn, the turf can be cut and peeled back to reveal the soil underneath. If the problem is a high spot, soil can be skimmed off and the turf rolled back into place. With a low spot, soil can be added to raise the level before replacing the turf. Always press the turf firmly on to the soil to give good contact and prevent the turf from drying out.

Opposite Gardening doesn't get much more instant than laying a lawn with turves. Wooden boards used as walkways help to protect the grass while firming it gently into position.

Above Departing from the usual squares and rectangles, the lawn here consists of two interlocking circles. They are complemented by the circular areas of hard landscaping and the curved beds.

Although not so hard-wearing as grass, low-growing aromatic plants can make very attractive lawns. The chamomile path shown here releases a delightful scent when clipped or walked on.

Pennyroyal (*Mentha pulegium*) also acts as an insect repellent, and is particularly good for deterring ants.

There are some disadvantages to non-grass lawns: the plants don't provide the close-shaven, smooth appearance achieved by a grass lawn, they are not as hard-wearing, and the leaves may turn brown at the edges in a hard winter. Also, weed control is difficult because some weeds, such as yarrow, are close relatives of the lawn plants, so this excludes the use of chemicals. Ironically, in a non-grass lawn the most difficult weeds to control tend to be fine-leaved grasses.

GROUND-COVER PLANTS

An aromatic lawn is an option, but not the only one. A small area of lawn could also be turned into an easy-maintenance flower-bed, using low-growing shrubs and grasses less than 45cm (18in) high. The plants will spread or creep over the ground. Different mulching materials, such as bark chippings or gravel 5cm (2in) thick, can be used to reduce moisture loss and suppress weeds.

To grow ground-cover plants through a mulch, mark where each plant will go and dig a planting hole large enough for the root system. Place a weed-suppressing membrane material over the entire bed, and stretch it as tight as possible by sealing the edges about 15cm (6in) into the soil. Cut an X into the material at the point where each plant will grow, folding the flaps back to expose each hole.

saying goodbye to the
LAWNMOWER

Lawns look good, but you don't have to have one. There are plenty of highly attractive alternatives, and some mean that you don't have to do any mowing.

A LAWN WITH NO GRASS

Before lawnmowers were developed in the mid-19th century, grass was not that popular, and gardeners often used other low-growing plants as a substitute. Today these lawns are making a comeback and are particularly useful if you want some sort of lawn but have only a tiny garden. What's more, since most cylinder mowers cut too closely for these plants and leave a 'ribbed' effect over the lawn, trimming can be done using shears or a rotary mower with the blades set at a height of 5cm (2in). Many of the grass-alternative plants have aromatic leaves that release a wonderful scent when they are mown or walked on.

Plants for a non-grass lawn

- Buttonweed (*Leptinella atrata*)
- Chamomile (*Chamaemelum nobile* and *C. nobile* 'Treneague')
- Convolvulus (*Dichondra micrantha*)
- Corsican mint (*Mentha requienii*)
- Pennyroyal (*Mentha pulegium*)
- Wild thyme (*Thymus serpyllum*)

These should be planted at 15–20 plants per sq m (sq yd). Small plants, such as seedlings or rooted cuttings, are planted at 30–40 plants per sq m (sq yd). They should cover the ground completely within 6–10 weeks of planting.

Low-growing shrubs (under 45cm/1½ft)

Calluna vulgaris (heather)
Genista pilosa 'Vancouver Gold'
Juniperus sabina 'Tamariscifolia'
Rosa x jacksonii 'Max Graf'
Skimmia japonica 'Bowles Dwarf'

Ground-cover plants

Cotoneaster dammeri
Geranium macrorrhizum
Hypericum calycinum
Luzula sylvatica 'Marginata'
Persicaria affinis (*Polygonum affine*)

WHAT MAKES GOOD GROUND COVER?

To be successful, ground-cover plants must have three qualities in order to suppress weeds and reduce maintenance. 1) They should be hardy and self-sufficient, needing very little care and being able to grow in poor conditions. 2) They should have a rapid growth rate so that they cover the soil within two years of being planted. 3) They should have dense enough foliage to prevent light from reaching the soil, which is why evergreens are often preferred.

For most herbaceous perennials used as ground cover, a plant density of 5–7 per sq m (sq yd) is ideal, but for most woody shrubs and conifers a plant density of 2–4 is fine.

Take the first plant by its stem or leaves, gently remove it from its container and place it through the material into the hole below. Backfill with soil, firm gently into place and water. Fold the flaps back around the base of the plant and continue until everything is planted. Hide the material by covering it with a layer of mulch such as gravel.

Although ground-cover plants reduce maintenance, they do need some attention once in a while to keep them healthy. Low, spreading plants tend to produce long, straggly growths if they are left to their own devices, and a good clipping, ideally every other year, will sort them out. Using hedge shears will encourage side shoots to develop, making the growths thick and matted and providing better cover. Some long shoots can be pegged down with wire to encourage them to root and form new plants.

Above For real low-maintenance gardening, cover open spaces with bark or gravel, which need little more than an occasional raking.

Right A clipped grass path runs through a meadow of long grass and buttercups: a traditional favourite with most gardeners.

WATER FEATURES

Adding water to the garden really brings it alive. Apart from encouraging wildlife, it is also wonderfully soothing on the ear and eye. You can have anything from a raised pond on a patio to a fountain, or an artificial stream using recycled water. The only limit is your imagination and how deep you're prepared to dig.

what's so special
ABOUT WATER?

Having a water feature adds an extra dimension, even to a small garden where space is limited. You can grow plants in and around the water and its presence will help to encourage wildlife into your garden. Water also has a wonderfully calming influence.

SITES FOR SORE EYES

As the *Ground Force* gardens show, there are endless ways of bringing water into your garden. There are ornamental ponds, miniature ponds in containers, wall-mounted and bubble fountains, waterfalls... and endless designs and ways of positioning them in your garden. You can have a water feature tucked away in a quiet corner, hidden from the rest of the garden by bamboos and tall wispy grasses, a place to sit and read. Or it can be a big, immediate feature with a formal, elegant shape or a strong, modern-looking design. It can even have thick, raised sides where you can stand pots of pelargoniums in the summer. Or you can have a small, cascading waterfall to transform a slope.

Ponds are an ideal way of completely changing the character of any part of the garden you simply don't know how to tackle. Generally, though, they are best when seen in context, when offering a contrast or change of emphasis. In small front gardens, for example, a pond can be rather one-dimensional. They are immediately bare and apparent, lacking any magic. But discovered tucked away in a clearing in the middle of a border, surrounded by pebbles and stones, they make a terrific surprise. Use ponds as a tool, as a way of delighting visitors.

If you want something extraordinary, you could even create one long, snaking pond, whose sides are hidden by vegetation, which runs alongside, then under, then out the other side of a miniature bridge or walkway. And you don't need a big garden to do this – just the vision, the effort, and the willingness to create large water features instead

The presence of water, whether moving or static, brings magic and tranquillity into a garden. No matter how large or small, a pond will attract wildlife and insects, often becoming a major focal point.

of conventional borders. The whole effect can be enhanced by hanging chiming bells from nearby trees.

Apart from their soothing influence, another advantage of ponds is that they act like mirrors. It's very easily forgotten, but the one thing all ponds do is reflect not just what's above, but what's behind them. The best way to test this out and make sure the pond is in the right place is to lay a large mirror on the lawn. The results can be quite surprising.

When choosing or siting a water feature, don't rush your decision. Look at examples in the very best gardens. Whichever style you choose, remember it should fit in with the overall feel of the garden. A formal design requires a symmetrically shaped pond edged with paving and constructed, perhaps, with the same materials as those used elsewhere in your garden. A more natural-looking country

Below A small, circular pond in a formal setting. The paving material used picks up the colour of the retaining walls, making the pond an integral part of the garden rather than an isolated feature.

Right With a surround that resembles organ pipes, this unusual pond makes a striking garden feature. Its design catches the eye, while its bubbling water soothes the spirit.

garden would benefit from a loose-shaped pond with lots of marginal plants to blend the edges into its surroundings.

Bear in mind, too, who's going to use the garden. Raised ponds make it easier for the elderly or infirm to see fish and plants without having to bend down.

BEGUILING THE SENSES

The first thing you notice about water is that it adds sound and movement, from sudden high-powered vertical jets to the constant dripping of a wall fountain. Even a still pond adds movement, with wind, insects and other creatures disturbing the surface. Make sure that wherever you site a pond there is space for people to look at it. You could even have a camouflaged seat if you're a keen animal observer.

THE BEST CONDITIONS

For pond plants to grow well there must be good sunlight for at least six hours a day, but avoid suntraps, which the fish dislike, and which lead to constant evaporation. At the other extreme, frost pockets are out, and you must avoid the shade of tall plants, and overhanging trees, whose falling leaves and vigorous roots can pose acute problems. Keep poisonous plants, such as yew and laburnum, well away.

MAKING A POND
the easy way

A pond adds interest to any garden, not least because it increases the range of plants that can be grown. The specialized micro-climate can play host to lots of wildlife.

Installing a pond couldn't be easier. You can either buy pre-cast pond shells, which come in different shapes and sizes, or pond liners for covering the inside of a hole. That's the good news. The bad is that the holes don't appear by themselves: you've got to dig them.

LINERS AND PRE-CAST SHELLS

The simplest option for making a pond is to use flexible liners because they are so easy to use. They can be made from a number of materials; generally, the heavier the gauge, the longer they will last. The liners can be moulded into any shaped hole and are easy to repair. They are great if you want a more natural-shaped pond than that provided by a pre-cast shell, and are also easier to put down (see opposite for how to lay one).

Flexible liners can puncture quite easily if laid too taut around the hole, but generally a top-grade plastic liner or a thicker rubber (or butyl) one will last around 25 years. They are considerably cheaper than pre-cast shells, and are used on the *Ground Force* programmes because of their many advantages.

Pre-cast shells come in predetermined shapes and sizes, and are made from plastic or fibreglass. Middle-of-the-range pre-cast shells will usually last around 15 years. While they don't puncture as easily as flexible liners, they can crack; the easiest way to repair them is by covering them with a flexible liner. The downside of shells is that the range of shapes and sizes is limited, they can look contrived and they tend to deteriorate more quickly than flexible liners.

POND DEPTH

When planning your pond, decide roughly what size it will be – not the shape, but how long, wide and deep. This is important for establishing the types and numbers of plants and fish that can be introduced. To support a wide range of plants and fish, the depth of a pond at its deepest point should be 60–90cm (2–3ft). This depth will provide adequate protection from predators and harsh winters, while providing an even, constant temperature throughout the summer. Ponds with less than this depth may still be adequate for the fish and plants, but there will be less of a buffer during extreme conditions.

MAKING A POND WITH A PRE-CAST SHELL

Mark out the shape of the shell with canes and dig out a hole 30cm (1ft) bigger than its shape. Put soft sand in the base of the hole to prevent the shell cracking. Place the shell in the hole and check with a spirit level that it is perfectly level. Fill the shell with water and at the same time cram soil in under the shelves and at the sides of the shell to secure it. Hide the visible edges with paving or turf.

HOW TO MAKE A POND WITH A FLEXIBLE LINER

1   Mark out the shape of the pond; if you want an irregular shape, a garden hose can be laid out until the shape is decided.

2   As you dig the hole to form the contours of the pond, remove the valuable topsoil and store it for later use.

3   As you dig deeper, leave ledges or shelves on which to position plants.

4   Check that the rim is level using a spirit level and plank. Some of the excavated soil can raise any low areas around the rim. Compact the soil inside the hole. Line the hole with moist sand or old carpets to prevent the liner from being punctured.

5   Unwrap the liner and lay it centrally over the hole. Pour a few litres of water on to it to act as a weight and drag the liner into the bottom of the hole, then it's off with your shoes and socks as you get into the hole and spread out the liner. Then fill up the pond with water.

6   Trim any excess liner around the rim, leaving about 15cm (6in). Hide and secure it with a layer of turf or a row of paving slabs.

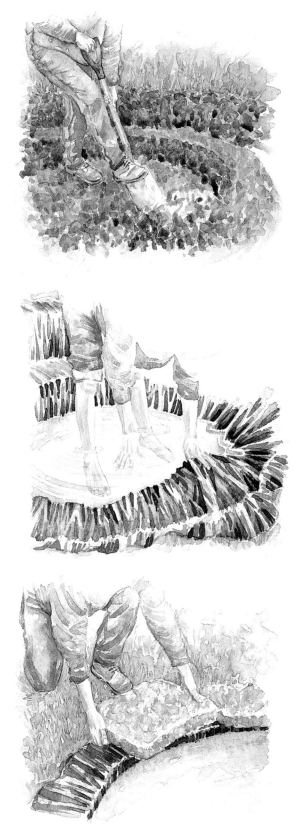

Calculating liner size for a pond 5m (16½ft) long, 3m (10ft) wide and 75cm (2½ft) deep
- Length of liner required = length of the pond + twice the depth of the pond
  (i.e. 5 + 1.5m (16½ + 5ft) = 6.5m (21½ft))
- Width of liner required = width of the pond + twice the depth of the pond
  (i.e. 3 + 1.5m (10 + 5ft) = 4.5m (15ft))
- Allow a little extra for folds and overlaps, so buy a pond liner of 7 x 5m (23 x 16½ft).

miniature
PONDS

You don't actually need a garden to have a small pond or water feature. It is easy to make a water feature in a container for a patio and stock it with a few plants and fish. Being manoeuvrable, it could even be moved indoors if the tender plants need winter protection.

BOWLS AND CONTAINERS

Any container that can hold water, even a wooden one that can be lined, has the potential to become a pool or pond. Unlike sunken ponds, the outside will be visible, so make sure it is attractive. You can use the container almost anywhere: to brighten up the corner of a patio, to add interest near the dining area, or to add an extra dimension among an arrangement of pot plants.

The larger the container, the greater volume of water it can hold, and the wider the range of plants and fish that can be used. A container should be at least 60cm (2ft) in width and depth if you want to keep fish, and for a container as small as this, goldfish are your best bet. Do bear in mind, though, that few plants grow well in rapidly moving water, especially when it is a small volume of water. Putting a fountain and aquatic plants close together is therefore difficult. Also note that large, saucer-shaped containers are better for small fountains; this shape will help reduce water loss resulting from drifting water spray.

MATERIALS

There is no real limit to the type of material from which the container can be made, and although waterproof materials such as moulded plastics, metals and glazed clay are ideal, other materials can be treated to hold water. Terracotta, reconstituted stone, porous concrete and wood can all be used, provided they have been water-proofed. Materials used for sealing ponds, and some bitumastic paints and coatings, will form a very good seal when applied to the inside of a porous container. A black interior to the

The sound of water trickling or running over stones is wonderfully soothing, and when it's combined with a fountain, you have a sight to please the eye as well.

Left Shallow water features can be made to appear much deeper if a dark lining or layer of gravel is used below the water line. In the example shown here, gravel and stones within the pool link with those used elsewhere in the garden.

Below Containerized water features, such as this wooden half-barrel, have one big advantage over fixed features – they can be used in different parts of the garden from year to year. Make sure that the plants you select correspond with the scale of the container.

container is preferable because it will absorb light, giving the impression that the water is deeper than it is. This is especially important when the container is relatively shallow.

LIGHT AND HEAT

Most aquatic plants prefer a bright, well-lit position in order to grow and thrive, but this in itself can be a problem because growing plants and keeping fish in fairly shallow containers in full sunlight can be an easy way to boil vegetables and poach fish at the same time. You must shade the surface of the water for at least a couple of hours in the hottest part of the day.

Quick freeze

Containerized water features are more prone to frost damage than garden ponds which have the surrounding garden soil as a form of insulation. They therefore freeze earlier in the winter and for longer periods. Break the ice very gently (if it isn't too thick) when fish are present (see pages 70–71) and to give birds a drink of water; alternatively, melt the ice with the base of a hot pan held on the surface.

Even the smallest of pools benefits from a thoughtful planting scheme. Here an interesting range of flower shapes and colours contrasts effectively with textured foliage and varied leaf shapes.

STOCKING
the pond

The size and depth of a pond determine the number of plants and fish that can form a healthy, balanced environment. Choose plants that won't invade your pond and add some oxygenating weed to keep the water clear.

SELECTING THE RIGHT PLANTS

One of the most difficult tasks is finding the right plants to fit the scale of the pond, and the smaller the pond, the more difficult the problem becomes. Where fish are present, some vegetation is essential. It provides food and cover from predators, such as herons and kingfishers, while also shading the water, helping to keep it cool.

It is important to have a mixture of plants within the pond because they all perform different functions. Waterlilies and deep-water aquatics, growing in depths of 45–60cm (1½–2ft), provide perfect shelter for the fish; oxygenators are important for the clarity and quality of the pond water; and bog plants (see pages 78–79) and marginals provide shade in the shallow water, where many young fish will congregate.

Floating plants provide cover on the water's surface but they can grow rapidly, blocking out the light and choking all other pond life. Introduce sufficient plants when you stock the pond to colonize only up to one-third of the surface area of the pond. As a rule of thumb, there should be about three plants of whatever kind per sq m (sq yd) of pond surface. Plants to avoid because of their tendency to invade include *Azolla caroliniana, Decodon verticillatus, Lemna major, Lemna minor* and *Sparganium erectum.*

PLANTING AQUATICS

Aquatics can be grown in basket-like containers, which are usually made of strong plastic (metal and wood containers can produce toxins which are harmful to fish). These containers make the plants more accessible for maintenance and propagation.

The plants which are to be submerged or partially submerged are planted in these mesh containers in the spring, using a special soil-based, aquatic plant compost which contains no fertilizers that will foul the water. The upper surface of the compost is covered with a 2.5cm (1in) layer of pea shingle to prevent the compost from floating away and making the water cloudy.

A basket can be lowered into the centre of the pond quite easily: thread a long length of string through its sides and tie the two ends together. You need an assistant to stand on the opposite side of the pond – both take hold of the string and lower the basket into the centre of the water until it settles on the bottom. The string can now be released.

FEEDING

Aquatic plants usually need feeding only every year or two. The most common means of feeding involves placing a pellet or sachet of slow-release fertilizer in each basket. This is done by fixing the fertilizer on to the tip of a long cane and inserting it where needed.

DIVIDE AND RULE

Many aquatic plants are propagated by division in the spring. The containers are lifted out of the water and all the compost is washed away from the plants before they are divided into smaller segments and replanted in new containers. The old central part of the plant should be discarded.

CHOICE HARDY PLANTS

The following plants are suitable for small and medium-sized ponds.

Deep-water aquatics

Aponogeton distachyos The water hawthorn has long, fleshy, light green, floating leaves, with highly scented cream flowers during summer, which turn green as they fade.

Sagittaria sagittifolia cv. **'Flore pleno'** This beautiful, fancy aquatic has light green, arrow-shaped leaves and white flowers with double rows of petals in mid-summer.

Orontium aquaticum This strange-looking plant has fine, pencil-like, yellow and white flowers held above the water on slender green stems. The blue-green leaves are lance-shaped and float on the water's surface.

Oxygenators

Callitriche species These plants are very similar to each other in appearance, having light green leaves which form a rosette on the surface. They grow well only when the water chemistry is well balanced, making them perfect indicator plants.

Mentha aquatica Technically a water purifier, the water mint has oval-shaped, dark green leaves with deeply toothed edges on purple-red stems. The small lilac flowers appear in small round clusters in summer.

Lagarosiphon major (Eloidea crispus) A submerged aquatic with brittle stems, densely clad with small, lance-shaped, deep-green leaves that curve downwards. Small tubular flowers, which are green tinged with pink, appear in summer.

Floaters

Hydrocharis morsus-ranae This pretty plant resembles a miniature water lily, with small, mid-green, kidney-shaped

Below *Mentha aquatica* is an excellent plant for growing in the shallows of a pool, but needs regular trimming as it can be invasive.

Above *Stratiotes aloides* is a strange-looking plant but it has attractive flowers and loves having its 'feet' wet. It's easy to grow and look after.

leaves. The small summer flowers each have a yellow centre surrounded by three white petals.

Stratiotes aloides The water soldier resembles the top of a pineapple floating on water. The cup-shaped female flowers are creamy-white with a papery texture, while the male flowers are carried in tight clusters in a pink, rolled-leaf-like structure; both appearing mid-summer.

Utricularia vulgaris Bladderwort has showy, bright yellow antirrhinum-like flowers that appear on long stalks above the water in mid-summer. The delicate, bright green foliage has a lace-like appearance, with small flotation bladders mixed among the leaves. Suitable for soft water areas only.

Marginals

Eriophorum angustifolium The cotton grass reaches 45cm (18in) and produces fine grassy foliage topped with fluffy white, cotton-wool-like flowers in early summer. Like all eriophorums, this plant must be grown in a water-logged, acid soil. It's invasive, so regular trimming needed.

Iris laevigata The blue-flowered aquatic iris with sword-shaped, smooth green leaves grows up to 90cm (3ft) high and forms clumps up to 90cm (3ft) across. There are numerous different-coloured forms.

Mimulus luteus This musk has green, rounded leaves and green stems up to 30cm (12in) high, which are topped with spikes of bright yellow, snapdragon-like flowers. It flowers all summer and can be propagated by division in the spring.

Summer-flowering water lilies

Nymphaea **'Gonnère'** In summer this plant has pure white flowers with double rounds of petals, which look like snowballs bobbing about in the water. The medium-sized leaves are a fresh pea-green colour.

Nymphaea **'Froebelii'** This popular free-flowering variety has dull purple-green leaves and deep blood-red flowers with vivid orange stamens.

Nymphaea **'Rose Arey'** Large, star-shaped pink flowers with a distinctive aniseed aroma. The leaves are bronze when young, turning deep green with a crimson tinge as they age.

FISH and wildlife

A pond allows for a range of fish to be introduced and encourages wildlife into the garden. Don't expect wildlife to appear overnight. It might take a full season before the pond comes to life, and you might need to add young frogs from a neighbour's garden. But when the pond is at full throttle, it becomes quite magical.

HOW MANY FISH YOU NEED

An ornamental pond doesn't have to have fish to be a successful feature, but to a certain extent it lacks activity and interest; adding fish to the pond immediately transforms it. If you buy fish when they are small, they'll establish better and they're cheaper of course.

The types of hardy fish that can live together in an ornamental pond include goldfish, golden orfe, rudd, tench and shubunkins. Golden orfe and rudd should be introduced in quantity, as they prefer to swim in shoals. Tench are among the shyest of fish, preferring to live close to the bottom of a pond, scavenging on insect larvae in the accumulated debris of the pond floor.

Young fish of all kinds might need to be temporarily removed to another site until large enough to fend for themselves. If the pond is overcrowded, the parent fish happily eat their young.

Ponds are an absolute magnet for wildlife. Some will visit regularly once or twice a day to drink and wash, while others, such as the frog, will take up permanent residence.

Above Many insects, such as this dragonfly emerging from a nymph, are drawn to water as part of their life cycle. They feed on and around water, but also provide food for other animals.

Right Koi carp are among the most popular fish stocked in ornamental ponds. They bring flashes of colour to dark water and provide an element of fun with their feeding-time antics.

When buying fish, check what size they will be when they are mature. This gives an immediate sense of how many you need. With most ponds an initial stocking rate is 5cm (2in) of fish, including the tail, for every 30 x 30cm (1 sq ft) of pond surface. Hi-goi carp and Koi carp should only be used in a pond made for them because they eat all plants and are too big for the average-sized pond. If used, they should be introduced at a rate of one fish for every 2.5 sq m (3 sq yd). Avoid mixing exotic fish with native varieties, as some of the latter eat exotic fish and their eggs. Never introduce exotic fish into lakes or rivers as these fish might carry diseases.

INTRODUCING NEW FISH

Place the container holding the fish on the surface of the pond to allow the water in the pond and the container to reach the same temperature. This will prevent the fish from suffering temperature shock when they are tipped into the pond. After 20–30 minutes open the container and tilt it into the pond water, allowing the fish to swim away. The fish will take 3–4 days to settle, after which time scatter some food over the pond surface or if you already have fish in your pond, carry on feeding as you would normally.

You might find your pool attacked by predators such as herons. Although unsightly, netting over the pool prevents your fish becoming food, and an imitation heron or two

placed around the water's edge can deter real ones; remember to move the imitation herons regularly.

In hot weather oxygen levels in your pool can drop and adversely affect the fish. Extra oxygen can be introduced in two ways: turn on the pool pump, if you have one. If not, flow water from a hosepipe into the pool. This disturbs the water's surface and creates oxygen bubbles.

HELPING WILDLIFE

To encourage wildlife, have at least one side of the pond sloping gently into the water. This will make it possible for small mammals and birds to drink and feed at the water's edge. As the pond and its surrounding area become established, the water will act like a magnet for newts, toads and insects, particularly those that feed on other insects. Most of the activity will take place from late spring through the summer months into autumn, with dusk being the busiest time of the day.

Hideaways

Most types of wildlife are relatively shy, especially in daylight. They can be encouraged to visit the pond by providing hideaways. This can be achieved by something as simple as a small area of weeds or wildflowers to provide cover, or a pile of brushwood or stones to make perfect hiding places close to the water.

troubleshooting
PONDS

Looking after a pond doesn't have to be a hassle. Problems can be dealt with quickly and efficiently if you know how, and there are measures you can take to prevent some of them occurring in the first place.

REPAIRING LEAKS IN FLEXIBLE POND LINERS

During the summer, when the weather is hot and dry, ponds will usually suffer a drop in the water level. A loss of 2cm (¾in) a week is quite normal but any more than that needs investigation. If the level drops sharply and always falls to the same point after refilling, it is time to look for a leak. The simplest way to locate a leak is to take out more water, reducing the level as much as possible. With luck a wet patch will form on the liner where water seeps back into the pond from the adjacent wet soil. If not, the liner has to be carefully and systematically examined until the leak is found.

Mending holes in a flexible liner is relatively easy, rather like mending a puncture in a bicycle inner tube, but it must be done in warm dry conditions to get good contact between the liner and the repair patch. Do not drain the pond completely if the hole is up to two-thirds of the way down the side of the pond; keep the fish and plants in 15cm (6in) of water while mending the hole. Leave the liner to dry before brushing the surface clean. Use a liner repair kit to mend the hole, cutting a patch from the repair sheet at least twice as long and twice as wide as the damaged area. Then clean the patch and around the hole with methylated spirit. You can now cover the patch and the damaged area with waterproof bonding adhesive. When it feels tacky, stick the patch on and press it firmly to ensure good contact. Placing a heavy weight over the

During the winter it's a good idea to keep a ball floating in a pond. Its gentle movement slows down the freezing process and prevents the surface becoming completely frozen.

repair will stop it lifting as the adhesive dries. Finally, check the repair after 24 hours, and if it is firmly bonded to the liner refill the pond.

LEAKS IN PRE-CAST SHELLS

If you find a leak in a pre-cast shell, your best option is to line the shell with a flexible liner. Empty out the pond and, when dry, follow step 5 onwards on page 65. This is a long-term solution, as the flexible liner lasts for about 25 years.

REPAIRING NON-FLEXIBLE POND LINERS

Most non-flexible pond liners are made of concrete, and leaks in them are generally the result of deep cracks caused by severe frost, or by uneven settlement of the pond. Tackle leaks by first removing any fish and plants from the pond, then empty it, leaving the concrete liner to dry. Brush away any dirt or debris. With a hammer and masonry chisel, chop out some concrete around the crack to make it wider, then brush clean. Force waterproof mastic cement into the crack, packing it tightly. Leave this to dry (according to the manuacturer's instructions) before painting the whole of the concrete lining with several coats of pond sealant. The pond can be re-filled the following day.

PREVENTING FROST DAMAGE

Frost is the most common cause of pond leaks. As water freezes and ice forms, it expands and the pressure can cause concrete to crack. Leaving a block of wood or a plastic ball to float on the pond's surface helps to prevent a solid sheet of ice forming and reduces frost damage with its slight, constant movement.

Charlie's Tips for Top Results

Apply a tonic treatment to fish ponds to keep fish in good condition, free from parasites and diseases.
Stop feeding fish in autumn when the water temperature drops below 6°C (43°F) and reduce sediment and foliage from the bottom of ponds to give fish more water space.

THE RIGHT KIND OF WATER

Few people have a natural spring in their garden, so the water for your feature has to be obtained from elsewhere. The best source is mains water but this can present a few problems. Domestic supplies have higher levels of mineral salts than occur in most pools, which may well increase the growth of algae. Also, the lime content of mains water is higher than in natural ponds. Consequently the acid/alkaline balance might need to be

adjusted to satisfy the needs of both plants and fish. You can do this by using chemicals, or by waiting two weeks or so before stocking your pond with fish. This period allows the level of mineral salts to come down, making the water habitable for fish.

The amount of algae can be reduced by placing a sack of straw or hay in the water. The straw or hay uses up oxygen as it decays, depriving the algae of nutrients they need, thereby restricting their development. If the water is too acidic (which is very rare), a small amount of limestone can be added to bring the pH up to 6.5. If the water is too alkaline (pH 9.0), a partial water change might help, provided the replacement water is not alkaline. Alternatively, add a pH buffering agent to the water. Take pH readings regularly and aim for a reading between 6.5 and 8.5; pH kits are readily available from most garden centres.

Left It may sound odd but it's true: a sack of hay or straw placed in a pond will absorb the nutrients that algae feed on. This will reduce the growth of algae and help to keep the water clear.

Above Unchecked, floating plants will eventually cover the surface of a pond, blocking out light and harming other plants and fish. Keep them under control by pulling out any surplus at regular intervals.

BUBBLE fountains

What about a water feature without a pond? You can still have noise and movement from even a small amount of water without the extra work that a pond involves. And an easily built bubble fountain is perfectly safe for young children.

MAKING A BUBBLE FOUNTAIN

In the aptly named bubble fountain water bubbles up through a group of pebbles or a large, flat stone (with a hole drilled through it) that's placed in the middle of a group of pebbles. This type of fountain can occupy an area as small as 30 x 30cm (1 x 1ft), with all the workings and equipment totally hidden from view. This gives the illusion that the water is rising up from nowhere, tumbling over the stones and vanishing.

A bubble fountain requires little maintenance. Some water is lost through evaporation, so check the level in the pool regularly (once a week through the summer, less often at other times) and top up when necessary.

SUCCESSFUL PUMPING

Most pumps come with a cable. You can also install a pump which uses mains supply electricity, as the *Ground Force* team do. Place the pump in the base of the pool and run the cable back to an indoor socket. Fix a circuit breaker into the mains plug: it cuts out the electricity if a fault develops. If any parts are damaged, return the unit to the supplier rather than trying to repair it yourself. (Also see pages 118–119.)

Pump sizes

Consider the following when choosing a pump:

1 The kind of feature it will serve, and whether it needs continuous or intermittent flow.
2 The height, or head, of the fountain or waterfall from the water surface.
3 The outlet – the type of nozzle.
4 The pond – the volume of water held in the pond at its normal capacity.
5 The pipes – their internal diameter, and the distance the water has to be pumped.

Left The running water here provides the humid conditions much loved by certain plants.

Right Pebbles are an attractive way of concealing the water tank hidden below.

HOW TO MAKE A BUBBLE FOUNTAIN

1   Start by digging a hole at least 25 litres (5.5 gallons)
    in volume to accommodate a reasonable reservoir
    of water and a submersible pump to circulate it.
    The easiest way to do this is to buy a small water
    cistern from the local DIY warehouse. This will have
    the volume of water indicated on the side.

2   Bed the water cistern on a layer of damp sand and
    use a spirit level to make sure that the rim is level.
    Pack loose soil into the gap between the outside
    of the cistern and the walls of the hole.

3   Put the pump into the cistern, making sure that
    the sealed electrical connections are not
    damaged. Set it to an appropriate flow setting
    before filling the tank with water to a level above
    the top of the pump. Test the pump to make sure
    it is working.

4   Cover the tank of water with a sturdy metal grid
    resting just on the soil surface), with the outlet
    spout of the pump protruding through it.

5   Cover the grid with a layer of pebbles to hide the
    top of the pump. Turn on the pump and
    reposition the pebbles as necessary to make a
    nice flow.

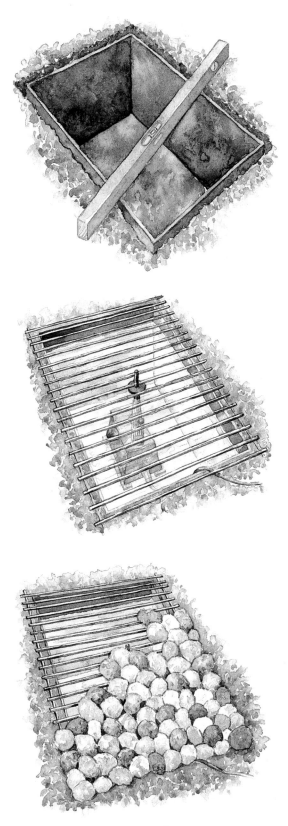

waterfalls and
FOUNTAINS

Garden centres sell a multitude of water features, all of which provide interest and variety. Many work perfectly well with or without a pond, and most are easy to build and maintain. However, whichever one you choose, remember to keep it in scale with the rest of the garden.

WATERFALLS

One of the most common misconceptions about even small water features is that they are difficult to install. But all that is required to have moving water is electricity to power a pump. No mains water supply is necessary, and a small reservoir of around 45 litres (10 gallons) will need topping up when the level drops – probably not at all in winter and once a week in hot weather.

A waterfall can range from a subtle change in level, with water flowing down a series of small, evenly spaced steps, to a large, dramatic change in levels, with higher volumes

Below Limited space needn't prevent you having a water feature. A wall-mounted fountain, for example, could be installed even on a balcony. In this small garden the sound of water falling into a tank draws attention to the feature.

Above Waterfalls don't have to be grand to enhance a garden. In this example two pools built at different levels provide an ideal opportunity to make a waterfall, which in the process turns two small features into a larger one.

of water causing a great deal of noise and making a strong, eye-catching feature. A waterfall can also be constructed to create a series of mini pools by tilting each level slightly back into the slope. Generally, the slower the speed of the water, the greater the range of plants which will grow in and around it.

WALL-MOUNTED SPOUTS

Gargoyle-like masks, animal heads or tilted vessels such as urns or watering-cans spouting water into a pool or pebble bed make marvellous additions to a garden. Usually a tank for the circulating water and a submersible pump are hidden behind the wall, or beneath the water outlet.

Charlie's Tip for Top Results

Always wash stones or pebbles thoroughly before using them in a pool. This gets rid of any surface lime, which may harm fish or raise the pH of the water. Buy a pH testing kit from your local garden centre and make sure you test the water at least once a year.

The humid atmosphere created by the gentle splash and spray of water is perfect for growing ferns and moisture-loving plants close by. Many water features can be bought in kit-form and are very simple to install.

FOUNTAINS

Some people feel that a formal pond is incomplete without a fountain, or a fountain-like ornament, gushing water back into the pond. Certainly the water droplets are an attractive sight as the sunlight plays on them. Jets producing too fine a spray often lack impact because the water outline is difficult to see from a distance, and the fine droplets drift in the wind, soaking surrounding surfaces and neighbours. The height of the spray should always be less than half the width of the pond to keep it in scale with its surroundings.

Pumps should be placed on a raised base of two or three bricks rather than on the bottom of the pond or vessel. Tie the pump to one of the bricks with a piece of wire as pumps tend to vibrate and sometimes move, which can result in the jet of water going in a different direction from the one intended. Placing a pump on a

In a sloping garden, a pool and waterfall not only make an interesting landscape; they also allow you to take advantage of the uneven ground rather than trying to level it.

raised base will also prevent the filter clogging up quickly with mud and leaves that gather at the bottom of ponds and fountains. Remember to clean the front of the pump when the water flow drops.

Watering-can folly

Some really interesting water features can be made by using recycled materials, such as an old metal watering-can (or several if you have them). Fasten the can to a wall or fence and install a small circulating pump inside it. Arrange it so that water fills the tilted can and pours out of the spout into a pebble-covered hole in the ground, from which it is quickly recirculated through a pipe back up to the pump. Alternatively, use two cans, with the water tipping and recirculating from one to the other. Simple and fun.

BOG gardens

If you have a constantly damp patch of garden, don't ignore it – turn it into a feature. There are plenty of plants that thrive in boggy conditions, adding to the range you can grow. If you'd like to create such a garden, it's easily done and is best positioned next to a pond. Marginal plants can of course be used beside your pond simply to make it look more natural.

HOW TO MAKE A BOG GARDEN

A bog garden can be any size you like, but the soil does need to be about 30cm (1ft) deep to allow the plants' root systems to develop. Some low spots in the garden can be used to form a natural bog garden, but on a free-draining site a plastic or similar waterproof liner will be needed to keep the area moist. Line the bottom two-thirds of the hole, leaving the top one-third free. If the soil becomes too waterlogged, the water seeps over the sides of the liner to the soil beneath.

Unless your garden soil is particularly poor, it should be kept for filling the liner because it will closely resemble the surrounding soil and be more compatible with it than any imported compost. Weeds, however, may be a problem in the early stages. For the best effect, a bog garden linked to an adjoining pond is perfect, with the overflowing water from the pond seeping into the bog garden. On the other hand, bog gardens work very well as stand-alone features.

THE BEST POSITION

This is invariably in dappled shade. Many of the plants grown here are herbaceous perennials which grow rapidly in the spring, producing large, soft tender leaves because of the damp conditions. This makes them susceptible to spring frosts and leaf scorch in hot, bright sun.

THE BEST PLANTS

The following list shows plants grouped according to their main season of interest. Choose a balance of those with all-year colour and ones with different flowering times.

Spring

Cardamine pratensis A perennial, producing tufts of fern-like foliage resembling green foam from a distance. The single flowers are rose-lilac and carried on stalks up to 45cm (1½ft) high in spring. The double-flowered form is *C. p.* 'Flore Pleno'.

Lysichiton americanum A clump-forming member of the arum family with bright yellow spathes which emerge in the spring, followed by large, coarse, cabbage-like leaves up to 1m (3½ft) long. Commonly known as skunk cabbage.

Primula denticulata The drumstick primula is a popular, spring-flowering plant with globes of small, purple flowers on thick, stocky stems 30cm (1ft) high. The green coarse leaves form an open rosette, and are often covered with a whitish dusty coating in spring.

Salix gracilistyla 'Melanostachys' A bushy shrub with a spreading habit, which eventually forms a thicket 3m (10ft) high and 4m (13ft) wide. The main feature is the black catkins and red anthers produced in spring before the leaves appear.

Summer

Aconitum napellus A plant with mounds of glossy green, finely cut foliage, with erect spikes of hooded navy blue flowers up to 1.5m (5ft) high in summer. Although it will grow in herbaceous borders, this plant performs much better in boggy conditions.

Astilbe chinensis pumila A low-growing, attractive plant with mid-green, fern-like foliage and spikes of tiny deep pink flowers on 15cm (6in) high stems in summer.

Hosta crispula An excellent foliage plant with lance-shaped leaves banded with streaks of white. In late summer the lilac-coloured flowers appear on slender green stems up to 75cm (2½ft) long. Prone to damage by slugs.

Mimulus cardinalis This plant has brilliant, scarlet-orange snapdragon-like flowers in late summer on 60cm (2ft) high stems, covered with pale green foliage. It prefers damp rather than wet soil, and may need some protection during winter.

Autumn

Aster puniceus The swamp aster has showy, daisy-like flowers which are pale lilac, carried on reddish stems in late summer and early autumn. The mid-green foliage has a rough, hairy texture, and the plant itself can be quite unruly, forming large, dense clumps up to 1.5m (5ft) high.

Eupatorium purpureum This tall, coarse-leaved plant grows up to 1.2m (4ft) high and produces crowded heads of purple, daisy-like flowers in late summer and early autumn. A vigorous plant which needs plenty of room.

Ligularia veitchiana An interesting plant with roughly triangular leaves and tall spikes of yellow, daisy-like flowers reaching up to 2m (6½ft) in late summer and early autumn. Does well in a partially shaded spot.

Primula florindae A giant primula with large heads of pendant, sulphur-yellow flowers carried on stems 1m (3½ft) high. The broad, coarse leaves are pale to mid-green, and the whole plant gives off a musky aroma.

Winter

Cornus alba The dogwood is grown mainly for its winter colour, deep red stems up to 1.2m (4ft) long, after the leaves have turned a sulphur yellow and fallen in the autumn. There are several variegated leaf forms, which also provide summer interest: *C. a.* 'Spaethii' has gold and green foliage, and *C. a.* 'Elegantissima' has green and white variegated leaves.

Salix alba 'Vitellina' The golden-stemmed willow produces new shoots up to 1.5m (5ft) long each year. They are covered in golden-yellow bark throughout the winter, but must be pruned hard each spring to produce this vivid effect. *S. a.* 'Chermesina' produces orange shoots in winter.

THE ECOLOGICAL BALANCE

Bog gardens must be regularly maintained to prevent any one species from overcrowding its neighbours and totally dominating the scene. In very moist soils plant growth can be extremely vigorous, so plants need to be lifted and divided regularly.

Any weeds, pests or diseases must be controlled using organic methods, not only because pesticides contaminate the water but also because many of the ornamental plants are close relatives of invasive weeds and using chemicals would kill both the weeds and the ornamental plants.

Left Looked at creatively, low-lying wet areas in a garden can be a source of opportunities rather than problems. A bog garden is ideal for poorly drained soil, and the plants that grow there can be positive assets.

Opposite Among the many plants that like wet 'feet' and have colourful flowers are primula, caltha and iris. But don't forget the wonderful shapes and textures provided by the foliage of water-loving ferns and hostas.

FEATURE COMFORTS

Decking, paths and walls have all been dealt with earlier in Structured Gardening. Here we deal with other garden structures that add privacy and practicality. Fences, sheds, screens and even gazebos all have a part to play in making your garden an attractive and welcoming place.

foundations and
BUILDINGS

Buildings and structures can contribute a great deal to the garden. Some are functional – sheds, summerhouses and greenhouses – while others, such as gazebos, pergolas, arbours and arches, are mainly decorative in purpose.

SOMEWHERE TO HIDE

Even the smallest garden requires a place to store equipment, such as spades, trowels and bags of compost, so that the garden does not become cluttered and messy. A shed is ideal for this. If you have enough space, you might consider building a summerhouse, creating a tranquil retreat from the pressures of daily life where you can enjoy the garden in peace. With an increasing number of people working from home, there is also a growing trend towards using summerhouses as home offices.

Most sheds and summerhouses are made from wood, and the most commonly used wood is deal. This is an umbrella term for a type of softwood and mainly refers to wood from pines and firs. Deal is susceptible to rotting, so always make sure that it has been pressure treated with preservative, and give it an extra coat of preservative yourself when you put it up. Other types of wood used include teak and cedar, which are costly but long-lasting. They need to be treated with teak or cedar oil. To ensure that sheds and summerhouses look in keeping with their natural surroundings, adorn them with flowering plants in hanging baskets or wall-mounted pots, or grow climbers on trellis or wires secured to the wall. Alternatively, use paint to brighten up the building, perhaps in a colour that echoes that of painted trellis elsewhere in the garden. Colours that look good include royal blue (for the daring), soft shades of greenish-blue and white.

WORK AND PLEASURE

Greenhouses are necessary for those gardeners who want to propagate their own plants. They are made with aluminium or traditional wooden frames. Choose a style to match your house and garden, remembering that wooden frames look attractive but require regular maintenance.

Gazebos, pergolas, arches and arbours can be used to give the garden a focal point, add instant height and provide a framework for climbing plants. A reasonable-sized garden is required for a gazebo, a decorative building that serves as a small, private garden room. Pergolas and arches can form a visual divide between one part of the garden and another, at the same time creating a 'doorway' through which a tempting view can be seen. An arbour with a seat provides a lovely spot from which to

Many gardeners consider a greenhouse essential because it allows them to grow a wider range of plants than is possible outdoors. When thoughtfully positioned, greenhouses can be attractive features in themselves.

look out on to the garden, especially when it is clothed with scented climbers. Pergolas, arches and arbours can be built easily by those who possess some woodwork skill, or you can buy wood or metal models in kit form.

POSITIONING BUILDINGS

Where possible, buildings and other structures should be sited to allow maximum light into the garden. If the site is exposed, it is tempting to use the building as a form of windbreak to provide some shelter, but this can lead to turbulence on the sheltered side of the garden. (The wind whips over and down.) Note that the best forms of windbreak are about 40 per cent porous and work by filtering the wind. In general a windbreak protects an area over a distance equivalent to about 10 times its height.

A greenhouse has special needs and cannot be placed just anywhere. Make sure that it receives maximum light levels, and position the axis running from west to east. The end of the structure should also face into the prevailing wind to minimize the area that gets a buffeting. This, in turn, limits heat loss and wind damage.

There will need to be some sort of a path to the greenhouse, and it's useful to have an area outside for hardening off tender plants as they acclimatize to colder temperatures. The greenhouse also needs to be well away from overhanging tree branches in case one snaps and breaks the glass – a very costly mistake. Also avoid frost pockets and shade. By positioning a greenhouse close to the house, it will be easier and cheaper to install electricity.

TYPES OF FOUNDATION

The kind of building and its function will dictate the type and thickness of materials used for the foundation. For buildings that need to carry weight, foundations of 15–30cm (6–12in) are common. Raft foundations made of a solid concrete slab are preferred, having the advantage of also providing the floor of the building. For storage buildings, those with a built-in floor with strong floor joists, or buildings erected on sloping sites, pillar

With their open sides, gazebos are a practical way of enjoying the garden, sheltered from the weather. They also provide background and support for containers and climbing plants.

Easy maintenance

Most building structures will require some repairs and maintenance during their lifetime, even if it is only a coat of paint or wood preservative every other year. This means that access will be needed to carry out these tasks. Always try to allow for this around all sides of a building.

foundations are often used. These are block or brick pillars set vertically on to level concrete pads so that the joists or base of the building rests on them. While this type of foundation may not be as good as a solid raft, it is quicker to build and discourages vermin such as rats from nesting underneath the building. For a greenhouse, a strip foundation, which runs along the length of a building, is often used to support the glass sides and framework, especially if plants inside the greenhouse are to be grown in the soil borders.

boundaries,
FENCES AND
SCREENS

Fences create a surround for your garden while marking a boundary between you and your neighbours and providing privacy. They are an instant, cheap solution if you can't wait for a hedge to grow, and are used on the *Ground Force* programmes because of this. No matter how good your garden, there are always some items in it that you would rather not see. Compost heaps, refuse bins and oil tanks are usually top of the list, and can easily be hidden with screens, which also serve to divide up a garden.

THE LEGAL SIDE TO BOUNDARIES

When a fence is to be erected along a boundary line, it is important to check the exact position of the boundary to prevent any disputes with the neighbours. The positioning of the supporting posts is therefore particularly important. With manufactured fences and screens, the height limit is usually 2m (6½ft) unless prior planning permission has been obtained.

TYPES OF FENCES AND SCREENS

Manufactured fences and screens have two major advantages over plants used for the same purpose: they provide instant disguise, whereas plants take time to grow, and they take up a specific area, unlike plants, which always take up more room to provide the same cover.

A good fence or screen should be a well-built, though not a solid, structure, and should act more as a wind filter than a barrier. Consider it a form of garden camouflage to disguise rather than obscure any unsightly items. The various types include chain link fencing, which is ideal for training plants along; interwoven wood; ranch or hazel hurdles, which are ideal for wind protection; and larch lap, which gives good privacy.

High walls can be oppressive, particularly in a small garden. Softening them with screens of climbing plants can create a feeling of intimacy without restricting the space below.

The more solid the structure, the greater its potential for blocking out sunlight and preventing adjacent plants from growing well in the shade it casts. However, structures that create partial shade are actually quite welcome. A wide variety of plants thrive in these conditions. An 'interlap' style fence, be it horizontal or vertical, is a good choice because it lets through light and gives good air circulation, while hiding an eyesore.

Wooden fences or screens can also be used to lead the eye in a particular direction or away from a certain object. This is most commonly achieved by arranging the cladding boards into an arrowhead so that the eye naturally follows the point of the chevron, or by using coloured paints and stains to draw attention to the fence or screen and away from its surroundings.

A cheap alternative to buying a fence is to make your own, either from old floorboards you might have or by buying secondhand ones. Hold the boards together with long floor joists running at 90 degrees to the floorboards. Remember to leave a small gap between each board to filter winds.

Above Hand-crafted fences and screens, such as these willow panels, lend a rustic feeling to the most urban of gardens. The fact that they are made from a natural, renewable resource also appeals to many gardeners.

Right Natural materials, such as bamboo, willow and hazel, make excellent screens. They take up very little room, age gradually as the new garden matures, and will last for many years before they have to be replaced.

Fences can give a boxed-in feel to your garden, so soften the impact by growing climbers along them (see pages 90–91). Climbers don't take as long to grow as hedges and they'll provide extra colour when in flower.

STEPPED FENCES

If you have a slope and want to put up panel fencing, you will need to make it stepped. Some posts will need to be longer as you work your way down the slope, so bear this in mind when you order the fencing. Note: fences made from different-sized panels don't work. Keep each panel the same size for an ordered, uniform look.

Protecting fences and screens

Manufactured fences and screens are usually treated with a wood preservative before they leave the factory, but if you are building your own screen with untreated wood, it is always advisable to use a preservative. Ideally, all wood should be re-treated either every year or every alternate year to give maximum protection against weather, paying close attention to areas at soil level or where the wood has been cut across the grain, such as the ends of posts. Good-quality wood which is well maintained should last for 15–25 years, with the more expensive hardwoods, such as beech and oak, having greater durability than softer woods, such as larch and pine.

erecting
FENCES

You can easily put up a fence yourself as long as there are two of you. Remember, fences don't stay up by themselves – they need extremely good supports. Everything you need can be readily obtained from your local DIY store. When they are well anchored and rigid, fences provide a terrific structural framework. The panels or boards should have a certain degree of flexibility so that they are not damaged by windy conditions.

SUPPORTS

Whatever the type of fence, they all need supporting posts, whether of concrete, metal, pre-treated timber or, less commonly, plastic. Traditionally, posts are inserted into a hole and bedded in with concrete, or held in place by compacting soil firmly into the hole around the base of the post. Increasingly they are bound by metal spikes with a cup fitting (see How to Erect a Fence opposite) because these are easy to install and relatively rot-free. Alternatively, on exposed sites, a pre-cast concrete spur can be bedded into concrete, with a wooden post then bolted on to the spur, which extends the life of the posts. Timber or concrete support posts should be at least 10 x 10cm (4 x 4in) thick to support a fence 1.5–1.8m (5–6ft) high.

It is important to check angles and levels at regular intervals when erecting a fence. Accuracy in the early stages of construction makes the work much easier and helps extend the life of a structure.

FOUNDATION DEPTHS

On a very windy site don't just increase the depth of the foundations or the thickness of the posts to cope with the weather – reconsider your choice of fence. A more open type of fence will offer less wind resistance than a more solid barrier, and will act as a filter.

The golden rule is to sink at least 25 per cent of the support post into the ground; therefore, a 2.4m (8ft) high post should have at least 60cm (2ft) buried, leaving 1.8m (6ft) above soil level. Wooden posts are most likely to suffer rotting within a 15cm area above and below soil level due to the constant changes of temperature and moisture on and around the soil surface. The consequent expansion and contraction leads to the wood fibres being damaged and accelerates the rotting process. It is therefore important to decide how the fence is going to be erected and supported, paying particular attention to the type and depth of foundations which will support the structure against any high winds. In exposed areas upright fence posts can be given extra support by bedding struts (which are simply small posts) into the soil and positioning them so that they join the support posts at an angle of 45 degrees. These are placed on the sheltered side of the fence so that the force of the wind is transferred directly into the soil.

> ### A stiff mix
> Where posts are to be bedded into concrete, use a stiff mix of:
>   1 part cement
>   2.5 parts sand
>   3.5 parts coarse 20mm (¾in) aggregate,
> adding just enough water to moisten the mix so that it will bind together.

HOW TO ERECT A FENCE

Most fences erected to provide screening and shelter consist of panels usually 1.8m (6ft) wide and anything from 60cm to 1.8m (2 to 6ft) high. The most common means of support are 10 x 10cm (4 x 4in) wooden posts. A post at least 2m (6½ft) long is needed for a 1.8m (6ft) high panel.

1   The first job when erecting fencing is to mark out the line of the fence with string and pegs, then to mark the position of each post (see Tommy's Tip below).

2   Knock in a fencing spike to hold the base of each post; for fences over 1.8m (6ft) high use 75cm (2½ft) deep spikes. Check that the spikes are upright, then fix the post into its socket.

3   When two posts have been erected, attach two panel brackets to each post, one 30cm (1ft) above soil level and one 30cm (1ft) below the top of the panel.

4   Slot the panel into place, check that it is level, and fix it into position. Cut the post down to 5cm (2in) above the panel, and fix a wooden cap on top of the post.

Tommy's Tip for Top Results

To mark out simply and accurately where each post should go, cut a 2m (6½ft) cane to a length of 1.9m (6ft 4in) to equal the width of a panel plus the thickness of a post. Lay this along the string line and knock a peg in at the end of the cane – this will be the centre of each post.

hedges and
LIVING SCREENS

The *Ground Force* team rarely uses hedges because instant results are required but they are worth considering if you intend to stay in a place a good few years. There is a wonderful selection of hedging plants to choose from, and although they take time to grow they will add dignity to any garden.

HEDGING YOUR BETS

Fences are great for small gardens where space may be an issue, but if you have room, hedges are a marvellous addition. They add life to a garden by attracting wildlife such as birds and butterflies, and provide a colourful living backdrop, particularly to the back of a border, where they act as a canvas against which to place flowering plants. A hedge or screen of mixed species, such as copper beech, green beech and holly, provides an interesting tapestry effect with plenty of seasonal interest, introducing autumn berries for the birds. You can restrict its height to as low as 1m (3½ft) in extreme cases; unpruned, the holly will reach 15m (50ft) and the beech 25m (80ft). You could also clip and shape foliage to create a bold, interesting structure, or snip out some windows to give views.

Conifers are a fast-growing alternative if you want a hedge quickly. They lose moisture rapidly, so water in dry seasons. Beware, though – conifers, and especially Leyland cypress, need regular clipping, so avoid them if you are a low-maintenance gardener. They have also been the cause of disputes between neighbours.

Plants can also be used effectively to screen off areas of the garden. The type of plants used will depend entirely on what is to be disguised but, if space is at a premium, select plants with a narrow upright habit. Evergreens are the best choice because they provide cover throughout the year – the last thing you need is a view of the refuse bin when you need cheering up in winter.

PLANTING

Most hedges and screens consist of a single row of plants spaced 30–45cm (1–1½ft) apart, depending on the species involved. On exposed sites, where shelter and protection are the primary reasons for growing the hedge, it might be necessary to plant a double row. This consists of two rows of plants about 40cm (16in) apart, with a distance of 30–45cm (1–1½ft) between the plants, and the two rows staggered to encourage even growth. Alternatively, a temporary screen of windbreak netting can be placed on the windward side of the hedge to protect the plants while they are young, helping them to become established.

PRUNING

An informal hedge is one that's allowed to grow quite naturally, and should be pruned rather like shrubs (see page 27). Formal hedges should always be narrower at the top than at the base. This makes pruning easier and encourages growth at the base of the hedge. When clipping a formal hedge always start at the bottom and clip up to the top. This will allow the clippings to fall away as they are cut, making it easier to see what you are doing. And use a garden line stretched tight between two posts to mark the level top to the hedge: this helps you create a nice, even line.

Why stick to privet or Leyland cypress for hedges? Combination planting, of beech and holly for example, is very effective, the different colours creating a tapestry effect during the winter.

There's no reason why flowering shrubs can't be used for hedging. Choose the right species, such as *Viburnum tinus* 'Gwenllian', and you'll have pretty scented flowers throughout the winter.

CHOOSING A HEDGE

The following chart is a summary of the varying features of 20 hedges. It might look complicated at first glance but it's quite simple to read. The numbers 1–10 along the top relate to the key and the letters Y, N, D and E refer to yes, no, deciduous and evergreen. If, for instance, you're looking to grow a small hedge that is scented and with coloured foliage, first check the key for the number corresponding to each feature, which in this case would be 9, 3 and 4. Then look down the columns under those numbers for a 'yes' and you'll see that *Lavandula angustifolia* is the hedge that fits the bill.

KEY

1 = narrow upright growth
2 = attractive flowers
3 = coloured foliage
4 = scented flowers/foliage
5 = berries/wildlife
6 = anti-burglar
7 = tall hedges 3m (l0ft) high and above
8 = up to 1.8m (6ft) within 6 years
9 = below 1.8m (6ft) within 6 years
10 = deciduous/evergreen

Suitable Hedging Plant	1	2	3	4	5	6	7	8	9	10
Berberis x stenophylla	N	Y	N	Y	Y	Y	N	Y	N	E
Berberis thunbergii 'Atropurpurea'	N	Y	Y	Y	Y	Y	N	Y	N	D
Carpinus betulus	Y	N	N	N	N	N	Y	Y	N	D
Chamaecyparis lawsoniana	Y	N	Y	Y	N	N	Y	Y	N	E
Crataegus monogyna	Y	Y	N	Y	Y	Y	Y	Y	N	D
Elaeagnus x ebbingei	N	Y	N	Y	N	Y	Y	Y	N	E
Elaeagnus pungens	N	Y	Y	Y	N	Y	Y	Y	N	E
Escallonia 'Crimson Spire'	Y	Y	N	N	N	N	N	Y	N	E
Fagus sylvatica	Y	N	Y	N	Y	Y	Y	Y	N	D
Fargesia nitida	Y	N	N	N	N	N	Y	Y	N	E
Griselinia littoralis	N	N	Y	N	N	N	Y	Y	N	E
Ilex aquifolium	N	N	Y	N	Y	Y	Y	N	Y	E
Lavandula angustifolia	N	Y	Y	Y	N	N	N	N	Y	E
Ligustrum ovalifolium	Y	Y	Y	N	Y	N	Y	Y	N	E
Prunus laurocerasus	Y	Y	N	N	Y	Y	Y	Y	N	E
Pyracantha coccinea	Y	Y	N	N	Y	Y	Y	Y	N	E
Rosa rugosa	N	Y	N	Y	Y	Y	Y	Y	N	D
Senecio 'Sunshine'	N	Y	Y	N	N	N	N	N	Y	E
Taxus baccata	Y	N	N	N	Y	N	Y	N	Y	E
Viburnum tinus	N	Y	N	Y	N	N	N	N	Y	E

gardening
UPWARDS

You might think that your garden is packed with plants and that there isn't room for any more; this couldn't be less true. There is plenty of what designers call vertical space. You can grow climbers up the house walls, up structures along the boundary, creating an 'aerial' hedge, and on structures inside the garden. Well-used climbers add an extra dimension.

ARTIFICIAL STRUCTURES

There are many different support structures which can be used for climbing plants. Arches, arbours and pergolas are as attractive as functional, but will usually need to be at least 2m (6½ft) high so that it is possible for a person of average height to walk beneath them. Obelisks can be placed in the middle of a border where they form an ideal support, or can be used as a frame to grow a climber through. If you're using an obelisk in a container, the obelisk should be no more than 5–6 times the height of the pot, or the structure becomes top heavy and might fall over, especially in windy conditions.

Walls and fences are equally good at supporting climbing plants, but additional structural support such as wires or trellis will be needed for most plants. Trellis is also ideal as a light dividing screen to break the garden into sections or 'rooms'. They can then be clothed with climbers

Left Garden structures can actually increase your growing space. Arches and obelisks, for example, provide support for climbing plants, while pergolas are ideal places for hanging baskets.

Below Evergreen climbers, such as this *Pileostegia viburnoides*, keep their leaves through the winter, have attractive flowers and are perfect for hiding unsightly objects in the garden.

to provide additional natural screening. Swags of rope tied to pillars are suitable for plants with quite flexible stems, but while they look good, they do involve a large amount of tying in, so beware.

It does not matter if the support is made of metal or wood provided that it is substantial enough to hold the weight of the climbing plants in full leaf. More important is the thickness of any support the climbing plant is trying to cling to. Most climbing plants prefer to grip on to circular supports up to 1cm (½in) in diameter.

LIVING STRUCTURES

Climbers are often trained up walls or along fences, but in nature most climbers naturally scramble over trees and shrubs. In fact, some plants appear to attract climbers. They are usually plants with an open framework, giving the climber some light while it is growing through the support, or trees with a high canopy, giving light around its base. The support method used by the climbing plant will determine which plant it can best grow over – those climbers with fine leaf tendrils prefer to climb on plants with fine foliage and small branches while the climbers with twining stems will clamber over any living structure. Climbers with aerial roots and sucker pads prefer walls and fences.

HOW CLIMBERS CLIMB

True climbers are those plants which are able to attach themselves to other plants and structures for support, using a number of different methods to help them.

Annual climbers, such as this *Lathyrus odoratus* 'Kiri Te Kanawa', are excellent for providing rapid growth. They add colour and extend the seasonal interest when other climbers have finished flowering.

CLIMBERS GROWING MORE THAN 5M (15FT) AND THEIR MAIN SEASON OF INTEREST

Plant	Season
Actinidia kolomikta	spring/summer/autumn
Campsis x *tagliabuana* 'Madame Galen'	summer/autumn
Clematis montana 'Rubens'	spring
Clematis armandii	spring *
Fallopia baldschuanica	summer
Lonicera japonica 'Halliana'	summer
Pileostegia viburnoides	summer/autumn *
Rosa 'Mermaid'	summer/autumn *
Vitis coignetiae	autumn
Wisteria sinensis	spring/summer

* = evergreen

Aerial roots These emerge along stems of climbing ivy and hydrangea, for example, and cling to structures for support.
Leaf tendrils Modified leaves ending in twisting tendrils, which wind around the supporting structure e.g. clematis and sweet pea.
Stem tendrils Modified stems ending in twisting tendrils, which wind around the supporting structure e.g. grape vine and passion flower.
Sucker pads Modified stems ending in a flattened disc, which adheres to the supporting surface e.g. Virginia creeper.
Twining stems Main stems that twist around a supporting structure e.g. honeysuckle and wisteria.

Climbers for scent

- *Actinidia chinensis*
- *Clematis armandii**
- *Clematis montana*
- *Holboellia latifolia**
- *Jasminum officinale*
- *Lathyrus odoratus*
- *Lonicera periclymenum*
- *Stauntonia hexaphylla**
- *Trachelospermum asiaticum**
- *Wisteria floribunda*

  * = evergreen

Climbers that tolerate exposed, cold and shady conditions

- *Akebia quinata*
- *Berberidopsis corallina**
- *Clematis montana grandiflora*
- *Humulus lupulus*
- *Hydrangea anomala petiolaris*
- *Lathyrus latifolius*
- *Lonicera* x *tellmanniana*
- *Parthenocissus henryana*
- *Tropaeolum speciosum*
- *Vitis coignetiae*

  * = evergreen

CLIMBERS GROWING LESS THAN 5M (15FT) AND THEIR MAIN SEASON OF INTEREST

Plant	Season
Ampelopsis brevipedunculata 'Elegans'	summer/autumn
Clematis alpina 'Francis Rivis'	spring
Clematis cirrhosa balearica	winter
Hedera helix 'Glacier'	all year
Ipomoea lobata	summer
Jasminum beesianum	spring
Jasminum nudiflorum	winter
Lonicera x *heckrotii*	summer
Rosa 'Penny Lane'	summer/autumn
Trachelospermum jasminoides 'Variegatum'	all year *

* = evergreen

caring for
CLIMBERS

Most climbers will grow for a long time (often 25 years or more), but they will only flourish if they are well cared for. This care starts with selecting a good plant and planting it well.

CHOOSING A CLIMBING PLANT

Most climbing plants are offered for sale in containers, and regardless of which climber it is, there are a number of things to look for. First, choose a plant with three or more strong shoots originating from compost level – this is more important than having one tall shoot. Avoid plants with obvious signs of problems, such as mildew or aphids. See if there are any roots protruding from the drainage holes in the pots, a sign of a good root system. And finally, check on the label to see what the ultimate size of the plant will be – make sure it is not too vigorous for where you intend to grow it.

PLANTING AGAINST A WALL

Walls usually have foundations that are wider than the wall itself, and walls often cast a rain shadow (i.e. leave an area that gets no rain). Consequently, planting a climber at the base of the wall can be the kiss of death. Ideally, any climber should be planted at least 30–45cm (12–18in) away from the base of the wall, with the planting hole being at least twice as large as the dimensions of the climber's container. Always plant the climber slightly deep so that the surface of the compost in the container is 2–3cm (1in) below the soil surface, and then apply a 10cm (4in) layer of mulch around the climber. This is particularly important for clematis, which like cool, moist soil.

For more vigorous climbers, such as Fallopia (Polygonum), vines or wisteria, a framework of strong wires fixed to the wall with vine eyes is better than using trellis. Usually the wires are fixed horizontally and arranged at 30cm (12in) intervals up the wall. The new shoots can be threaded between the wall and the support wires and tied into position with a natural fibre string, such as hemp, which will rot within three years and prevents the tie constricting the plants' growth.

PLANTING UNDER A TREE OR SHRUB

For most climbing plants this is an even more difficult situation than planting against a wall as the climber is competing with its support for water. The best approach is to plant the climber midway between the main stem of the

supporting plant and the edge of its leaf canopy. This will allow a reasonable amount of light to get to the climber, while reducing competition between the two competing sets of roots. Again, the climbers will benefit from being mulched, but leave a slight depression close to the base of the climber to allow water to accumulate and seep down to the rootball.

Trees that support climbers

- Apple
- Norway maple
- Magnolia
- Gleditsia
- Laburnum
- Pine
- Yew
- Hawthorn
- Birch
- Cupressus

Shrubs that support climbers

- Azalea
- Juniper
- Rhododendron
- Euonymus
- Heathers
- Weigela
- Ribes
- Forsythia
- Cotoneaster
- Dogwood

Left Though not true climbers, climbing roses, with their beautiful, scented blooms, are excellent for training over walls, fences and pergolas.

Right Wisterias that flower in late spring and early summer can provide dramatic displays, but they do need lots of room. Pruning should be done twice a year to get plenty of flowers.

MAINTAINING CLIMBERS

The training and pruning of climbing plants are usually combined operations, with the key to correct pruning based on the flowering period and method of self-support. For plants such as wisteria, the aim is to control the growth of strong vigorous shoots so that more of the plant's energy is directed into flower production. The flower buds are produced on short spurs of growth, and more spurs are produced on branches that are trained horizontally. With many climbing plants it is advisable to remove all the dead flowers you can reach, as this prevents the plant producing seed and usually results in more flowers.

ROUTINE PRUNING

With established plants, the easiest approach is to prune twice each year. The first pruning is carried out in the summer, when the new, long lateral growths are cut back to just above a bud, 15–20cm (6–8in) from the point where they emerge from the stem. Other shoots intended to form part of the plant's framework are tied into position and left to twine around the supports. The second pruning

Trachelospermum jasminoides, an evergreen climber with scented flowers, is ideal for growing close to a window so that the scent can drift indoors.

is in late winter, when all of the summer-pruned shoots are cut back to form spurs consisting of 2–3 strong buds, which carry the flowers.

RENOVATION PRUNING OF CLIMBERS

Neglected climbers soon become a tangled mass of woody stems, and produce very few flowers. If the plant is healthy and vigorous, the best approach is to prune very hard to rejuvenate it. Most climbers will tolerate being cut back close to the base or back to the main framework of stems.

Cut down the plant to 30cm (12in) in the early spring, and as the new growth develops, train it over the support system. Those plants which are not healthy and vigorous may not survive such harsh treatment, in which case carry out the renovation pruning gently in stages over a two or three year period. Remove the oldest stems each year. To find out if a climber can withstand severe pruning, cut back a part of it to see how it responds.

Wall maintenance

One of the most popular ways of growing a climber is using a supporting trellis attached to a fence or wall, but this can present problems if the wall or fence needs regular maintenance. The best approach is to fix the base of the trellis to the wall with hinged fittings and to use hooks at the top. This allows the trellis to be unhooked and laid down if necessary. If a 3cm (1in) space is left between the trellis and the wall, the main stems of the climber can be trained into this space, and any side shoots will grow out through the trellis into the light.

CONTAINERS

No garden is complete without containers. They are a brilliant way of adding scent and flowers to parts of the garden where there aren't any beds, and perfect for growing plants when you've only got a balcony. Lilies, strawberries, ivies, lettuce – you name it, you can grow it in containers.

why CONTAINERS?

Containers offer fantastic advantages. They let you grow tender plants that wouldn't survive outside in the winter and are a great way of introducing instant colour, which can be moved about with ease to create different arrangements. Although they need constant watering in hot, dry summers, there's no doubt that containers give gardens lots of extra interest.

FREEDOM TO GROW

There are no limits to what you can achieve when growing plants in containers. It is, without doubt, one of the most versatile types of gardening because, depending on the size of the container, it is possible to grow plants almost anywhere. Anything that will hold compost, from a pair of old welly boots to a smart stone urn, can be used to grow plants, and the choice of container personalizes the planting as much as the choice of plants.

You can grow whatever you want, where you want, because the choice of plants is not limited by the soil type. The compost can be chosen to meet the needs of the individual plant, which in turn offers freedom of choice to grow a wider range of plants.

Another great advantage is that the planting can be changed as often as you like. A beautifully clipped miniature conifer, for example, could provide a permanent focal point, while a collection of herbs next to the kitchen door could be changed seasonally to meet all your culinary needs.

One of the main attractions of gardening in containers is that you do not need a garden at all – a patio, balcony or roof garden will do perfectly well, provided it will take the weight. The root restriction caused by the confines of a container is often seen as a problem for growing healthy plants, but the opposite is true. Large plants can be kept under control. And while containers do limit development by restricting root spread, when the roots fill the container there is a natural tendency for the plant to produce more flowers. As long as

Microclimates

During hot weather, container plants can be moved closer together to shade one another, reduce moisture loss and prevent drying out. Pot plants also look better in groups. The mass of foliage and flowers hides the pots and gives a more luxuriant, abundant feeling.

Left Container gardening can turn the most unfriendly or limited space into a vivid and inviting area, and it doesn't have to cost a fortune. The colourful display shown here consists largely of inexpensive narcissi and azaleas.

Opposite above Using brightly coloured pots that contrast with the planting inside them makes a bold statement, particularly in small or neglected areas that are unsuitable for permanent plantings.

Opposite below Containers are ideal for filling corners or dividing up open spaces. As the plants they contain come to the end of their flowering or foliage display, they can be removed and others brought to the fore.

the plant is well fed, there shouldn't be any problem with its health. This restriction also works well for extremely invasive plants, such as mint, by keeping them under control.

When plants become pot-bound and it's no longer practical to re-pot them into larger containers, the best approach is to remove the plant, knock some of the compost from the roots and refill the container with fresh compost.

Charlie's Tip for Top Results

To make large container-grown plants manoeuvrable, mount them on castors or small wheels. You can glue the wheels on to terracotta, concrete, plastic or thin metal pots; thicker metal ones will need to have holes drilled first. For wooden pots, screw the wheels directly on to the bottom. Use wheels big enough to support the weight.

MOBILE PLANTS

Plants growing in containers are not fixtures, so provided they are not too large, they can be moved around the patio or garden to create different scenes and soften the edges of hard landscaping. Container-grown plants can also be moved into prominent positions as they come into flower, while those that are past their best can be shunted into the background. Remember, it is important to turn container plants regularly to ensure that they grow evenly and keep a balanced shape.

The mobility of containers makes it possible to grow even tender plants because they can stay outside for the summer, then be moved indoors to avoid the worst of the cold weather. This means you can grow some of the exotic plants, such as bougainvillaea and plumbago, that you usually see only in Mediterranean countries, or even tender shrubs or small trees such as an orange or a lemon tree, which would give you your own supply of fresh fruit.

going to **POT**

Part of the fun of growing pot plants is choosing or making attractive containers. They are a terrific way of livening up the garden and stamping your personality on it. They let you be as traditional or eccentric as you like.

CHOOSING CONTAINERS

The range of container materials includes plastic, wood, terracotta, metal, wicker, concrete and stone, but some materials are better than others. Although often frowned upon, plastics have several advantages over other materials because they are light, durable and non-porous, which means that they do not require watering as frequently as those that lose moisture through their sides. Although wooden barrels might look more attractive, they have some inherent disadvantages: they tend to be heavy and dry out quickly, especially when the wooden slats shrink, leaving spaces between them. One way of overcoming this problem is to line the inside with a sheet of plastic, but leave the base uncovered to allow free drainage.

CONTAINERS FOR FUN

The only limit to the range of things that can be used as containers is your imagination. Almost anything can be recycled as a container, including old sinks, painted cans, wheelbarrows, plastic pipes, chimney pots and even old

Stability

Ideally, containers should have a broad base in relation to their height. In fact the broader the base, the more stable it is likely to be. This is particularly important when tall plants are being grown in the container, and when the container must stand in an exposed position. To give added stability, fill the bottom of the pot not with polystyrene chips or just a few rocks (to improve drainage) but a layer of heavy stones. The layer can be as deep as you like, provided the plant has the right amount of compost.

Be bold in your choice of containers and you'll double the interest of your display. Here a terracotta elephant stands next to a lush growth of parsley, while cascades of plants emerge from its back.

Left Small pieces of broken mirrors and shards of colourful glass and china can be glued to the outside of your pots to make vibrant containers unique to your garden.

Above Plain terracotta pots can be painted to contrast with or complement flowers and foliage growing inside. Use water-based paints to allow the terracotta to 'breathe'.

boots and sacks. Some of these might last for only a couple of seasons, but they'll add an element of fun while they're around. Bear in mind, though, that there can be drawbacks to using unusual containers. Those made of wood or metal might have contained substances that are harmful to plants, so it is essential to clean them thoroughly before planting up. You can then treat the inside with a bitumastic paint to act as a barrier between the container and the compost. Wait about one week after this treatment before putting in the plants.

CONTAINER SHAPES AND PROPORTIONS

Stand back and consider before committing your plants to pots. A broad, shallow container, for example, might hold a wide range of plants in a variety of colours, but this shape is possibly the worst. Its shallow depth combined with a large surface area exposed to the elements means the compost will dry out quickly. Far better, and less labour-intensive, are tall containers with narrow tops. They also look quite elegant.

MAKING YOUR OWN

You don't have to be a dab hand at DIY in order to make your own containers. Simply cut some wood to the appropriate shape and size, and stick the pieces together with waterproof glue. (You can knock in a few panel pins if you like to hold things together while the glue dries.) Nail or glue some small blocks of wood to the base to act as 'feet', then drill some holes for drainage. Finally, treat the whole container with wood preservative to ensure that it lasts for several years. If you prefer, simply make a colourful wooden casing and slip a plain plastic trough or container inside it.

LIVENING UP CONTAINERS

Home-made or home-decorated containers can be adorned with plastic or cut glass beads or small squares of mirror, especially if you want to give a Mediterranean feel to your garden. Mirrored surfaces are particularly useful for plants growing in shaded areas as they reflect light and brighten things up as much as containers painted in colours. Make sure you use water-porous paints on your pots, and don't be afraid to experiment with patterns: hoops and stripes always look good.

Ageing containers

To make new metal containers look like they've been in use for years coat them with a layer each of metal priming paint, mid-brown-coloured acrylic paint, olive acrylic paint and finally a light green acrylic paint.

planting
OPTIONS

There is a huge range of plants that can be grown in containers – everything from large architectural shapes to trailing carpets, from bright, hothouse colours to muted pastels. Getting the right appearance can be tricky but, by following a few basic rules, you can create an eye-catching feature.

STRONG, INTERESTING SHAPES

Many plants, especially when grown together, will just form a loose mound of growth and tend to lack interest and individuality. Where mixed rather than single-specimen plantings are used in a container, a mixture of tall, bushy and trailing plants provides an interesting combination. Nodding ornamental grasses, palm-like cordyline and spiky yucca are all capable of adding a new dimension to any planting scheme. Similarly, ornamental onions, agapanthus and foxtail lilies are terrific in containers because they produce flowers on tall, slender stems which stand proudly above the surrounding foliage; from a distance they can look like a floral firework display.

HIGHER AND HIGHER

The obvious way of adding height to a display is to incorporate some climbers, but these will give height only if they are supported. Artificial structures will do that job, but climbers often look better if they are supported by other plants. Tall flowers, such as lupins, lilies or foxgloves, make the perfect support for annual climbers, such as ipomoea and sweet peas, which climb over the dying flower stems and flower after the support plants have ended their display. This type of climber will also trail over the edge of a container, giving a softening, foamy effect.

GAP-FILLERS

These are the 'packing material' in any plant display, designed to give colour and interest while the other plants are reaching maturity. They are usually noticed only when they are in flower, which may be for a relatively short period. By the time they are waning, the principal specimens in the display will have filled out and taken over

Colourful gap-fillers (spring bulbs)

- *Chionodoxa luciliae*
- *Crocus tommasinianus*
- *Hyacinthus* 'Jan Bos'
- *Muscari azureum*
- *Narcissus cyclamineus*
- *Narcissus jonquilla*
- *Narcissus* 'Tête-à-tête'
- *Pushkinia scilloides*
- *Scilla sibirica*
- *Tulipa* 'Unicum'

Left Slightly tender plants, such as this pot-grown phormium, are often better suited to containers. The advantage is they can be moved to a warmer place when cold weather hits.

Above Low-growing plants can be displayed in raised containers. The ornamental grasses here also prefer the slightly drier conditions offered by growing them in containers.

the gap-fillers' area. Annuals are ideal as fillers because they tend to flower relatively early before dying away.

TRAILING PLANTS

Even the most attractive container can be obtrusive, and at least part of it should be obscured to hide the rigid lines and angles. As they increase in size, plants impart a softening effect, but this can take time, especially if small plants are used initially. The answer is to use trailing plants which will cascade over the sides of a container, quickly covering it. They will also provide shade, thus reducing the root temperature of the plants inside. Fast-growing plants such as bacopa, lamium, lobelia and glechoma will spread and trail very quickly, so are ideal for this purpose.

SCENTED PLANTS

Most container-grown plants are positioned close to the house or along pathways, where they can be appreciated as much for their scents as their appearance. Among those with particularly aromatic foliage are lavender, rosemary and scented-leaved geraniums. Their fragrance is released in hot, sunny conditions, but they need to be touched to provide the strongest aroma, so are best placed beside paths where people and animals can brush past them. Other fragrant plants tend to produce the strongest scent when their favoured pollinating insect is most active. Honeysuckle, for example, will smell sweetest in the evening when moths are in flight; similarly, many spring bulbs, such as hyacinths, are heavily scented to attract the few active insects around at that time.

Changing the colour theme is a great way of injecting new interest. Next year the trellis could be painted red and new plants placed in the pots, making this corner look completely different.

QUICK CHANGES

Despite having overtones of modern disposable culture, 'plunging' is a traditional gardening technique which can be very useful in the modern garden, where a fast change-round from one display to another is desired. For short-term displays, annuals and bedding plants grown in small pots can be inserted, pot and all, into larger containers. This method has three advantages: 1) there is no check in growth when the plants are transplanted because the roots are not disturbed; 2) when they have finished flowering, the plants can be easily removed by gripping the pot and giving it a twist to sever any roots that have grown through the drainage holes; 3) the plants can be quickly replaced with other, more attractive specimens.

exceptional
PLANTS

Whether you live on a windswept coast, rugged moorland or in the heart of a city, you can create any landscape you want with relative ease – as long as you do it in miniature.

One of the advantages of containers is that you can create the ideal conditions for plants with special needs. Mediterranean plants, alpines and even tropical species can all flourish outside their usual habitats. For example, you might not have room in your garden for a rockery, but you can create one in an old sink or a wide pot.

MAKING AN ALPINE TROUGH

Creating a miniature alpine landscape sounds like a tall order, but it's really very easy. The ideal container – an old stone sink – is something that most people would be happy to recycle, especially if it makes an attractive addition to the garden. By adding a suitable coating, it is possible to hide its kitchen origins and make it resemble natural stone. Start by cleaning it with a wire brush and detergent so that it's free of all loose dirt. Paint each side in turn with a bonding agent to make the artificial stone mixture stick. When tacky, the outside of the sink is then covered with a stiff paste consisting of equal parts of sand, peat and cement bound together with a little water. This covering should be at least 1cm ($\frac{1}{2}$in) thick. Leave it to dry for two or three weeks before planting up.

POSITIONING AND PLANTING THE TROUGH

As a stone sink is very heavy, put it in position before filling it with compost or plants. (Don't try to move it on your own – it's a two-person job.) Choose a site that's sheltered from the cold and out of the path of north and west winds. Ideally it should face south or west. Keep the sink away from trees and overhanging foliage so that other plants won't drip on to the alpines – they don't like it. Good drainage is very important, so rest the sink on brick pillars and tilt it slightly towards the plughole.

You'll probably find it best to plan your planting scheme on paper first. It's usual to grade the plants according to height, but this depends on how the finished

sink will be viewed. If it can be clearly seen from all sides, you might prefer to have height in the middle and graduate down towards the edges. If it's against a wall or fence, you might like to graduate the height from the back.

Miniature conifers are an attractive way of adding height, and you can plant a selection of miniature bulbs in among your chosen alpines so that you have a colourful and interesting display all year round.

Once you are happy with the final position of the sink and know which plants to use, fill it by placing a layer of broken clay pots or pea shingle in the bottom; usually 7–8cm (3in) is sufficient. Next fill the container with a free-draining compost (equal parts of John Innes No. 1 and fine gravel) to within 5cm (2in) of the top of the sink. Using a trowel, plant the alpines in the compost and cover the compost surface with a 2.5cm (1in) layer of gravel. This prevents the soil drying out and the roots getting too hot. It also prevents the plants being disturbed during watering or heavy rain.

ACID-LOVING PLANTS

Camellias, rhododendrons, pieris and ericas all have one thing in common – they love acid soil. Many people long to grow some of these beautiful ericaceous (acid-loving) plants, but think they can't because they don't have the appropriate soil. The simple solution for these gardeners is to fill a container with ericaceous compost and plant their favourite acid-lover in that.

Above Don't fancy an old kitchen sink in your garden? Just follow the advice on preparation, positioning and planting and you'll quickly forget its origins.

Right Whatever your soil type, you can grow almost anything if you create the right conditions. Acid-loving azaleas will thrive in containers filled with suitable compost.

growing
UP AND DOWN

Eye-level interest can be created in a number of ways. Perhaps the easiest and most striking effects can be achieved with colourful hanging baskets, pot-grown flowering climbers and cleverly clipped topiary.

HANGING BASKETS

There's no reason why beds, borders and knee-high containers should hog the limelight. You can surround yourself with colourful seasonal displays just by raising your sights a little higher. Hanging baskets can be used to liven up the dullest section of wall or fence, bring new life to gloomy corners and provide the brightest of welcomes next to a front door. All too often, though, they are under-used, with many being planted only for high summer. This is a shame because ivies, heathers and skimmia will produce an excellent display in winter and early spring, providing a perfect backcloth for displays of spring bulbs and seasonal plants such as pansies. The advantage of using hardy or perennial plants is that you can transfer them to the garden when you want to make a new look for your basket.

PLANTING UP AND WATERING

As with most jobs, preparation is all-important, so start by making a list of everything you'll need. Remember that hanging baskets always look best when tightly packed with plants, so don't be tempted to skimp. Choose those that will give you a pleasing variety of heights, shapes, colours and forms.

Sit your empty basket over a bucket, then line it with moss or a moss substitute. Add enough compost to fill

Hanging baskets make excellent use of 'dead' space. They can bring life and colour to empty areas where permanent planting may not be possible.

one-third of the basket. Insert the first layer of trailing plants by poking them through, roots first, from the outside. Add another layer of compost and repeat the process just described. Add the last layer of compost, insert the final trailing plants as described, then plant up the top of the basket with your chosen selection of plants.

Finally, fill the bucket with water and let the basket sit in it for an hour before hanging it up. Thereafter, regular and generous watering from the top is essential to keep hanging baskets looking good. You'll need to do it twice a day during the summer.

GOING UP!

Pot-grown climbers flourish perfectly well in containers, provided they are regularly fed and watered. Once established, you can train them to your desired shape. To create a plant with a standard stem usually 1.8m or 6ft high, train the main stem up a cane or similar support, removing any side branches each winter to leave the stem clear. When it reaches 1.8m (6ft) in height, remove the tip during the winter months so that new shoots can develop from the top buds. In the third winter, cut these shoots back by one-third to encourage a balanced top. In subsequent years, prune during the summer by cutting the new shoots back to 6cm (2½in).

Plants suitable for hanging baskets

Trailing	Upright
• *Convolvulus sabatius*	• *Artemisia*
• *Hedera helix*	• *Chrysanthemopsis gayanum*
• *Helichrysum petiolare*	• *Helianthemum*
• *Lysimachia nummularia*	• *Impatiens*
• *Thunbergia alata*	• *Pansies*
• *Verbena tenuisectax*	• *Pelargoniums*
• *Vinca minor*	• *Scilla mischtschenkoana*

CLIMBING AIDS

Support for climbing plants comes in two forms – either artificial (man-made frames or structures) or natural (other plants, either dead or living). Many forms of tripod-like structures, trellis or frames are available in kit form, or are quite simple to make from canes or large-mesh chicken wire. The most important point is to avoid using thick materials or objects for plant supports, especially when growing annual or tender climbers, as they are unable to twine around thick posts or poles.

Evergreen plants, such as pyracantha or certain species of ceanothus, also make good natural supports for annual or herbaceous perennial climbers, as they offer a degree of frost protection through the winter.

Man-made frames are available in all shapes and sizes, from simple arches for climbing roses to animal outlines for adventurous topiary.

INTERESTING CLIMBERS

Cobaea scandens Large, bell-like flowers, green and violet-purple, height 4.5m (15ft); tender perennial.
Eccremocarpus scaber Small, tube-like, orange-red flowers, height 1.8m (6ft); frost-hardy perennial.
Ipomoea hederacea Large, trumpet-shaped flowers which are deep blue with a white centre, height 4m (12ft); annual.
Lapageria rosea Long, hanging bell-shaped flowers, light pink in colour, height 2.1m (7ft); frost-tender evergreen.

Below Container-grown climbing plants are ideal for hiding unsightly features, brightening up bare walls and softening hard edges of patios.

Above It's easy to clip your shrubs and hedges into the shapes of animals, especially if you grow them through pre-formed wire frames.

Lathyrus odoratus The sweet pea produces large flowers in a range of colours from white to deep burgundy red, height 2.7m (9ft); annual.
Lonicera splendida The Spanish honeysuckle has small, yellow, tube-like flowers, height 1.5m (5ft); hardy evergreen.
Passiflora caerulea Spectacular, large, saucer-like flowers, with greenish-white sepals and purple filaments in the centre of the flower, height 4m (12ft); frost-hardy, evergreen in mild winters.
Tropaeolum peregrinum Unusual yellow petals, said to resemble an insect in flight, height 2.4m (8ft); tender annual.

TOPIARY

The art of clipping shrubs into ornamental shapes is known as topiary, and you can have a lot of fun with it. Start with something simple, such as clipping a pot-grown box or bay tree into a ball-shape. After a bit of practice, the sky's the limit: you can create barley-sugar twists, stars, or even immortalize your cat.

Many garden centres sell differently shaped wire frames that you simply place over the bush you want to clip. Position the frame when your plant is still small enough to sit inside it. As it grows, you simply trim it to the shape provided by the frame.

Plants suitable for topiary include barberry (*Berberis darwinii*), bay (*Laurus nobilis*), box (*Buxus sempervirens*), Chinese holly (*Osmanthus delavayi*), privet (*Ligustrum delavayanum*) and yew (*Taxus baccata*).

growing your OWN

The only thing that beats growing beautiful plants is being able to eat what you grow. It's easy to set aside a small area for a vegetable plot, but even balconies and window boxes can be successfully pressed into service as mini market gardens. It just takes a little planning.

VEGETABLES

They might be nothing much to look at, but grow-bags do their job very well. They are excellent for growing glorious summer produce such as tomatoes, peppers and aubergines, and they save you the bother of buying large pots and bags of compost. As a bonus, you can even use them for a second season to grow salad plants, such as lettuces, radishes and onions, which feed on the fertilizer residue from the tomato crop.

When growing tomatoes, bush types such as 'Red Alert' and 'Sleaford Abundance' are ideal as they will not grow higher than about 1m (3ft), need little support and do not need to have their side shoots removed. These plants should not be planted outdoors until the minimum night temperature is above 10°C (50°F). Fruiting usually starts about 20 weeks after the seeds are sown.

To produce your own new potatoes, begin in mid-spring by filling the bottom quarter of a bin bag with loamless multipurpose compost. Gently press the seed potatoes into it before covering them lightly with more compost and watering well. When the shoots are about 23cm (9in) tall, add more compost until only the tips of the shoots are visible: the shoots will continue to grow and the tubers will be ready for harvest when the shoots begin to turn yellow. The average bin bag will produce 7.5–13kg (15–25lb) of new potatoes, depending on which cultivar is

Herbs grown on a windowsill or out on the patio are easy to harvest fresh. Although many are strictly seasonal, some varieties can be grown all year.

grown. They will keep well if stored in paper sacks raised off the floor. Discard any rotten specimens as they will contaminate the others.

Many leafy salad crops, such as lettuce, endive, radicchio and rocket, are easy to grow. Simply sow thickly in a grow-bag, window box or large container and pick as required. If you cut off the leaves just above ground level, they will grow again to give a second crop.

HERBS

Many sun loving, Mediterranean herbs dislike rich, fertile soils, preferring poor, stony ground to snake their roots through. You can easily create these conditions by mixing equal parts of John Innes No. 1 compost with coarse grit to create a free-draining compost containing small quantities of fertilizer. Small herbs such as basil, coriander and parsley can be sown directly into this type of compost

Support for tall growers

Tall plants, such as aubergines, cucumbers, peppers and tomatoes, will need some support to keep them upright. For grow-bags where the compost is shallow, a wooden tray made from plywood with a border of timber, measuring 10 x 5cm (4 x 2in), nailed around the edge is useful. Holes are drilled into the two ends of the tray to hold the bamboo canes in, and string is run between them, so supporting the plants' stems. The whole structure is made stable by the weight of the grow-bag holding down the frame.

with 4–5 seeds in a 15cm (6in) pot. Garden mint prefers a damper compost and is very invasive, so it needs different treatment. Cut the bottom off a 30cm (12in) plastic pot and plunge it in the garden to two-thirds of its depth. Fill it with peat-free compost, then plant the mint in it. The container will prevent the mint from invading the surrounding area. Other herbs, such as bay and rosemary, can be trained into standard plants (see page 105), then trimmed into balls, cones or other shapes.

FRUIT

Most varieties of fruit can adapt to growing in containers, but there's little doubt that strawberries are best suited to this treatment. With their trailing habit and succulent fruit, they are perfect for hanging baskets and window boxes, but they must be kept well-watered to produce large berries. Cultivated plants such as 'Elsanta' and 'Pandora' usually do better in a loam-based compost such as John Innes No. 2. The trailing runners that develop after flowering can be trained into small pots of compost to make new plants. Simply rest them on the soil and peg them down. Once they have rooted and are making new growth, sever from the parent. When the parent plants become less productive after 2–3 years, use their 'young' as replacements.

Below Strawberries like growing in tall containers. The fruits are less accessible to birds and make a pretty sight hanging clear of the foliage.

Right Fig trees grow like weeds unless their roots are restricted, so they are best grown in pots and moved to protect them from the cold.

Growing figs in tubs

Given their freedom, fig trees will grow to 7.5m (25ft) high. However, grow them in a container about 50cm (20in) across and 75cm (26in) deep and they will reach only 1.5m (5ft) high. Figs like a slightly alkaline compost which is fertile and deep. Although they prefer a warm, dry climate, sheltered conditions, or a south- or west-facing wall, they grow very successfully in northern latitudes, but in exposed areas the whole tree needs to be covered with fleece to protect the young fruits from frost. Water the trees in dry summer periods, or the fruits may drop prematurely. They must be allowed to ripen on the tree. Pick when the flesh yields to gentle pressure when squeezed between finger and thumb. Pruning should be undertaken in early spring. Cut out any frost-damaged wood, as well as the old fruited wood, and prune back any weak young shoots to a single bud to encourage new shoots to develop.

Tender plants do not enjoy frosts and chilling winter winds, so keep them indoors until the worst of the weather is over. A greenhouse is ideal for over-wintering plants and giving an early start to those that naturally flourish later.

There are two basic types. Loam-based compost contains a proportion of soil, but in a balanced mixture which is more suited to plants that will be in a container for a long period of time. It is heavy but won't dry out too quickly, and holds its nutrients better than most composts. Loamless composts, usually based on composted bark or coir (coconut waste), are light and more convenient. These are especially good in large containers, and on roof and balcony gardens where weight is a consideration, but they do tend to dry out very quickly in hot weather.

WATERING AND RETAINING MOISTURE

The problem with composts that dry out very quickly is that they can be difficult to rewet. Using moisture-retaining additives will help to overcome the problem. Water-retaining crystals, added to the compost before planting up, can absorb vast quantities of water, becoming a gel in the process. As the compost dries out, the water in the gel seeps back into the compost, where it is made available to the plants. Most of these additives have a lifespan of one growing season.

There are several things you can do to prevent drying out in the first place. One is to cut the bottom off a plastic bottle, leave the cap half-unscrewed and invert it

care and
MAINTENANCE

Pot plants are entirely dependent on us for their survival. Tucked up in an artificial environment, they quickly suffer as nutrients in the soil are soon flushed out. Looking after container-grown plants used to be time-consuming, but now there are some short cuts.

TYPES OF COMPOST

Garden soil is generally totally unsuitable for containers because it can harbour too many weeds, pests and diseases. It also tends to slump and become compact as a result of the frequent watering that container-grown plants need. This impedes drainage and the roots tend to die due to a shortage of oxygen. That's why you need to buy potting compost at garden centres.

The right growing medium
Research scientists at the John Innes Institute created the well-known potting composts which were designed to be uniform in ingredients, consistency and quality. The two loam-based composts most commonly used are:

John Innes seed compost – consists of 2 parts sterilized loam, 1 part peat and 1 part sand with added fertilizers and lime.

John Innes potting compost – consists of 7 parts sterilized loam, 3 parts peat and 2 parts sand with added fertilizers and lime. This formulation comes in three strengths: the standard mixture is John Innes No. 1, but the amounts of fertilizer and lime are doubled to make No. 2, or trebled to make No. 3.

Easy feeding

To avoid the drudgery of carting cans or buckets of feed around to your plants, you can now buy a gadget that attaches to your garden hose. Called an Easy Feeder, it is a see-through beaker in which you place solid or liquid fertilizer. Screw on its cap, connect it to your hose and a dilute solution of liquid fertilizer is metered out into the water as it cascades over your plants. More expensive fertilizing systems have a dial which can be adjusted to regulate the concentration of fertilizer being released.

into a container of compost. Fill the bottle with water and it will trickle slowly into the compost, where it is taken up in small quantities. Alternatively, and particularly with large containers, mulch the surface of the compost with a light-coloured material, such as pea shingle, to reflect heat.

DRAINAGE AND FROST PROTECTION

Almost as bad as starving container-grown plants of moisture is making them waterlogged. This is particularly bad news in winter, as it will allow the soil to freeze all too easily. There are several ways to avoid this. Always ensure that your container has drainage holes in the bottom. If it hasn't, drill some (in metal or terracotta); with plastic containers, you can make holes by using a red-hot poker. Once there are enough holes, place a few broken crocks over them to keep them clear of soil. For extra protection, stand your containers on 'feet' to keep them off the ground. During really wet weather, you can cover the surface of the compost with a sheet of polythene; weight it down around the main stem with large pebbles and tie the outer edges around the pot.

If you have container plants susceptible to frost that are too big to bring indoors, you can protect them by making a 'wigwam' of canes and covering it with straw.

FEEDING FOR FLOWERS AND HEALTH

The roots of plants growing in containers rely on you to supply all their nutritional needs, so use an appropriate fertilizer to promote the kind of growth you want. Nitrogen promotes leafy growth, phosphates help roots to develop and fruit to ripen, and potash encourages flower and fruit development.

It is important to feed the plants little and often to reduce the chance of high levels of fertilizer burning the

roots. Always follow the manufacturer's instructions. Slow-release fertilizer sticks (called plant pins) can be inserted in the compost when planting up and will release nutrients gradually, but only when it is warm enough for the plants to start growing.

LOOKING AFTER TOPIARY

The more intricate the shape, the greater the amount of maintenance required. The secret of good topiary shapes is to trim little and often. You'll also find it easier to use secateurs or scissor-type shears rather than full-size hedge shears. There's less chance of lopping off something vital if you work with small tools.

Beautiful displays of some plants, such as this *Dahlia Hybrids* 'Bishop of Llandaff', can be made to last longer by removing dead flowers regularly.

gardening
IN THE AIR

Gardens can be made almost any-where, and this one proves the point. From this angle, it is impossible to tell that this roof terrace is several floors above street level in a bustling city.

The last thing you expect to see on top of a building is a roof garden, but they are becoming increasingly popular. They can be startlingly spare and minimalist, or thicket-filled cottage gardens. Whatever the design, they need plenty of thought.

PRACTICAL CONSIDERATIONS

Weight is the first major consideration. The combined weight of the containers, the compost when soaking wet, the plants, their supports, flooring and furniture must all be added up.

Check with a structural engineer on how sound your roof is if you think the extra weight might be a problem.

The plants on roof and balcony gardens need something in which to grow, and on an exposed site this is particularly important for anchorage. The compost has to be nutritious for the plants and light enough to avoid causing structural problems to the fabric of the building.

About 98 per cent of the water that the plants need must be provided by some form of irrigation, be it a watering can or a sophisticated trickle system with a

Climbers suitable for roof gardens

- *Campsis radicans*
- *Clematis armandii*
- *Eccremocarpus scaber*
- *Humulus lupulus* 'Aureus'
- *Ipomoea lobata (Mina lobata)*
- *Lathyrus latifolius*
- *Trachelospermum asiaticum*
- *Wisteria sinensis*

timing device (rain is never enough). Surplus water must be able to drain away freely without damaging the building's structure, or causing any stains.

SHELTER AND SUPPORT

It is essential to provide shelter and support for any rooftop plants in order to prevent them from being blown over and damaged. The wind is always more apparent several storeys up, and the problem can be even worse in towns where the buildings act as funnels, increasing wind speed up to six times that in open areas without buildings. Remember that the shelter you provide for the plants will also protect you from the wind – and from prying eyes – so think carefully before you create any fixed structures.

To make a good growing environment for the plants, the best solution is to create a mixture of natural screening and artificial shelter. Grow climbers up trellis or canes, have plants such as bamboos that will tolerate windy conditions, and erect screens of willow, hazel and bamboo. These materials might seem flimsy, but their strength is in their flexibility. They can bend with the wind, provided they are firmly but not rigidly anchored.

SUITABLE ROOF PLANTS

By their very nature, roof and balcony gardens are exposed to the elements, suffering any extremes of heat and cold that the weather brings. This means that there is a limit to the range of plants that can be grown there. Choose those that naturally grow in exposed, windswept conditions along coasts and on moorland, such as sea holly (*Eryngium maritimum*) and heather (*Calluna vulgaris*). Plants with silver or hairy leaves are a good bet because they don't lose too much moisture through evaporation and they reflect hot sunlight.

Roof-top survivors

Silver-leaved plants

- *Astelia chathamica*
- *Artemisia canescens*
- *Cynara cardunculus*
- *Dianthus* 'Doris'
- *Lavandula spica*
- *Raoulia australis*
- *Senecio cineraria*
- *Teucrium fruticans*

Hairy-leaved plants

- *Convolvulus cneorum*
- *Nepeta mussinii*
- *Salvia argentea*
- *Santolina neapolitana*
- *Senecio* 'Sunshine'
- *Stachys olympica* 'Byzantinus'
- *Thymus lanuginosus*
- *Verbascum olympicum*

Left Plants with reflective leaves, such as *Artemesia ludoviciana* 'Silver Queen', are ideal for growing in roof gardens, which have heat reflected from surrounding buildings.

Above Some plants, such as *Stachys byzantina* 'Silver Carpet', have hairy leaves able to trap and hold moisture, even in dry, windy conditions: good for a draughty roof-top garden.

GARDEN EXTRAS

With a little imagination and effort, a garden can be turned into a room outside, a sanctuary furnished to serve you and your family's needs. Here's a quick guide on how to get the best out of your garden, using lighting, garden furniture and other accessories.

the room
OUTSIDE

Making the most of the garden means using it as an outdoor 'room' – a place where it is possible to eat and relax in tranquil surroundings, and in which children can play. Of course, this room, like any other, requires furnishing, and its multi-purpose nature means that there are lots of considerations to be made.

BARBECUES

If you enjoy al fresco eating, a barbecue is essential. It needs to be partially sheltered, but positioned to allow easy access to both the kitchen and the eating area. Do not situate barbecues close to windows, as smoke will billow into the house. Also keep them away from any wooden structures where they would be a fire hazard. For safety, it is

Left Home-made barbecues can be made out of many things. This oil drum has been cut in half horizontally, painted and placed on brick pillars so that it's at a convenient height for cooking.

Below Static, brick-built barbecues are the ideal solution for those who eat outdoors frequently. This particular one has been designed to complement the paving on the patio. Planting at each side softens the edges of the brick.

best to place the barbecue on a level surface and at a height that is comfortable to work at. It is also a good idea to install lighting nearby so cooks can see what they are doing and thus avoid accidents.

TYPES OF BARBECUES

There are many free-standing or mobile barbecues that take up little space in the garden, and can be conveniently dismantled and packed away for the winter. These are particularly useful for small gardens. On a roof garden or deck, a lightweight mobile barbecue is a better choice than a permanent type, although one fuelled by bottled gas can be a problem as you have to carry gas bottles up and down stairs. For regular outdoor meals, a permanent, brick or stone barbecue, or one built using a sturdy metal container, such as an oil drum, is more practical. Whichever materials are chosen, the style of barbecue you decide on must be easy and safe to use. For example, in exposed gardens, a partially enclosed, oven-like structure with a chimney will help to disperse the smoke and give better control of the fire.

An interesting hybrid is the loose-brick barbecue, in which bricks are stacked together without mortar, and with a 5cm (2in) gap between them. The structure can be easily dismantled and the bricks stacked in a corner over winter. About 100 bricks are needed to create a decent-height barbecue (1m/3½ft), with a cooking surface sufficient for four people.

Always consider the size of grill and, where possible, choose one larger than necessary for your requirements.

This ensures it will be large enough to cook not only for the family, but for additional guests too. Finally, the cooking grill for any type of barbecue should be sturdy and well-made, but most importantly (and often not considered) it must be easy to remove for cleaning.

SAFETY FIRST

Always keep children well away from a lighted barbecue and be patient if the fire seems slow to get going. Do not be tempted to add too much lighter fuel.

GARDEN FURNITURE

A vital part of an outdoor room, garden furniture adds style and comfort. The first consideration is the size of the garden, bearing in mind that even the smallest garden should have somewhere to sit down and relax. If space is really limited, portable seats, such as foldaway chairs, can be stacked against a wall when not in use.

Take into account the garden's style, too, and choose furniture that will complement it – crisp, white-painted wrought ironwork in a smart town garden, for example, or rustic-style, wooden furniture in a wild cottage garden. (If you choose wooden furniture, ensure that it is treated with preservative to prevent it from rotting.) Garden furniture need not be a major purchase; think about the timeless appeal of a hammock strung between two trees – fun and often inexpensive, and a chance to brighten up the garden by introducing a splash of fabric colour.

Position tables and chairs near to the kitchen so that there is not far to walk carrying platefuls of food. Garden

seats, on the other hand, may be best placed near a scented plant, such as a rose or jasmine. Alternatively, if the garden is quite shaded, you might want to place seating in the spot that gets the most sun. Do not overlook the decorative merit of garden furniture either – a bench could provide a focal point at the end of a path, or a pretty chair enliven an otherwise dull corner.

CHILDREN'S PLAY AREAS

An outdoor play area allows children to release energy and have fun. In a large garden there are few limits and you can, for example, make use of a lawn in summer by putting up a net for games of badminton. More permanent features could include a swing or even a tree house. In smaller gardens there will usually be space for features such as a sandpit, a paddling pool or Wendy house. Play areas are best situated close to the house so that it is possible to keep an eye on children in case of accidents.

Above Peaceful retreat or hive of activity? Most gardens do duty as both, particularly if you have children. To reduce wear on the lawn, place a piece of artificial turf under the swing.

Right Children love sandpits, but you might find that the neighbourhood pets do too. A waterproof cover will keep a sandpit clean and allow the children to play in it even after heavy rain.

garden
LIGHTING

A circular bed with a central tree is accentuated by uplighters to create a dramatic focal point within a brick patio. The eating area is illuminated by soft candlelight.

Artificial lighting makes it possible to enjoy the garden in the evenings, when it can not only show off features, such as pretty statues or striking architectural plants, but create mood. Used skilfully, it can produce the same effect as natural light and also help deter burglars.

FUNCTIONAL LIGHTING

Some lighting is designed to be functional as opposed to decorative, being used to increase safety rather than create atmosphere. For example, lighting paths, driveways, steps and doorways is a practical measure to increase security. Beware

of introducing a bright floodlit effect, however, which casts deep shadows and is therefore counter-productive.

Many companies now produce lighting kits suitable for use in gardens, and these come with comprehensive instructions. If in doubt, hire a qualified electrician to install your lighting.

DECORATIVE LIGHTING

Well-designed garden lighting brings a special beauty to the garden at night, highlighting the best features while drawing attention away from any eyesores. Three different types are available. Downlighting illuminates features or areas of the garden from above. It can imitate nature, suggesting filtered sun or moonlight, when the light is directed through a tree or structure, casting soft shadows on the ground below. Uplighting directs light up from ground level and can be used to create subtle shadows, throw an outline into sharp relief, silhouette a subject or provide a focal 'glow' in the garden. It can create the most dramatic lighting effects but is best used sparingly. For the really ambitious gardener, underwater lighting can be installed in wall or bubble fountains to give a subtle effect that can look wonderful.

Diffused lighting, which scatters the light, should be used in preference to a bright floodlight, which produces glare and ruins an atmosphere of relaxation. Bright light also shortens the garden by creating deep shadows away from the light source, and the areas and features that are lit by floodlighting appear flat and uninteresting.

For those interested in wildlife, who perhaps encourage creatures such as birds, hedgehogs, frogs, toads and attractive insects into the garden, soft lighting can be an excellent aid to watching them. This is especially true if dimmer switches are used to raise the light levels gradually in areas where the wildlife feeds.

Insects are drawn towards light, so the further light fixtures are situated away from main seating areas, the less likely annoying insects, such as wasps and mosquitos, are to become a problem. In fact, positioning a source of blue light at the furthest point of the garden is a useful means of drawing insects right away.

LANTERNS, CANDLES AND NIGHTLIGHTS

Garden lighting does not have to be provided by electricity; oil-fuelled lanterns or lamps, and candles of all sizes look attractive and create soft, atmospheric pools of light, with a gentle, flickering effect achieved by a protected flame. Simply placing candles or nightlights in empty jam jars or terracotta pots arranged in rows or small groups is economical, and they look very pretty when lit. Small metal lanterns for holding candles are practical, too, and can be hung on wall hooks, well away from babies and small children. The smell of scented candles or scented oils is very pleasant, and some also act as insect repellents – an important consideration on a warm summer's evening.

Above Downlighting, which produces a soft, natural effect, is used here to draw attention to a stunning display of lilies planted in a large terracotta pot.

Right Abandon tradition and be inventive with candleholders. Some garden candles contain insect repellent, which can be a bonus on summer evenings.

The functional nature of this lamp is softened by the climbing rose, which has used the fixing bracket for extra support. The beautiful flowers will give a dappled shade effect when the light is turned on.

basic
ELECTRICITY

As the garden has become more of an outside room filled with lights, garden furniture and barbecues, so the need to have electricity out there has increased. If you're confident of setting up and working with electrical appliances, you can easily do it yourself; otherwise it's best to call in the professionals.

SELECTING CABLES AND FITTINGS

The power for garden lighting and electric motors can be a low-voltage supply connected to the mains electricity via a transformer. Although there may be some loss of energy, the low voltage is safer than running a system direct from a mains supply. The transformer can be positioned either on an outside wall in a weatherproof box, or placed indoors close to the power supply. It will usually have a mains cable connected to it. Then it's usually a case of following the manufacturer's instructions to connect the low-voltage cable to the transformer, before switching on the power. Use only cables and fittings of the correct standard and loading.

There are numerous submersible water pumps and garden lighting kits which are manufactured overseas and imported into the UK, but it is safer to use products which have the British Standard 'kite' mark on them. Unlike imported products, these are approved and guaranteed to a minimum standard. If in doubt about anything electrical, always consult an approved electrician.

Although most garden lighting is powered by low-voltage cables, many water features (including those used by the *Ground Force* team) are powered by mains electricity, especially where a more powerful electric pump is required to move water at higher pressures. Where mains electricity is used in the garden, a circuit breaker must always be used to isolate the outdoor appliances should they develop a fault.

LAYING AND DISGUISING CABLES

Always try to hide cables and disguise fittings. This isn't just easier on the eye – it's safer because there are no wires to trip over. Cable should be buried in a trench at least 20cm (8in) deep, running in the most direct route from the appliance to the power supply. It is also advisable to run the cable through plastic ducting pipe to protect it from any damage. With garden lighting, the power supply cables are sometimes laid on the surface and covered with garden mulch (this is only safe where no digging will be done in the borders). Alternatively, cables are run overhead to a post or tree, but care must be taken if any pruning is to be carried out close by.

A practical tip for compacting trenches where cables have been laid is to refill them with soil, then turn on the hose pipe to wash the soil down into the trench. This is a useful way of getting the soil to settle quickly without having to compact it using pressure. In fact, pressure can be dangerous in stony soils, where cables and ducting can be

Safety check
Many systems are available in kit form, with clear instructions, and can be installed by unskilled persons, but it is better to have an electrician check the work, just for safety's sake. Often larger schemes must be installed by a qualified electrician.

Circuit breakers
When running an electrical appliance from a mains supply, insert the plug into a circuit breaker. If a fault develops, it immediately cuts off the supply.

damaged by sharp objects if the soil is firmed down forcefully.

At least once each year all the electrical fittings and connections should be inspected to ensure that the weatherproof seals are in good condition. Any damaged fittings and seals should be replaced to reduce the risk of corrosion damaging units, necessitating their replacement.

WATER POWER

To install a low-voltage pump to power a water fountain (see pages 74–77), simply place it in the base of the pool. These pumps are usually sealed units and are perfectly safe, but if any cracks are noticed in the casing, or cables and fittings appear frayed or split, return the unit to the supplier. Don't try to repair it.

Security spotlights can be partially hidden by using plants as camouflage. Don't be tempted to have very bright lighting – this creates deep shadows, which are ideal hiding places for uninvited guests.

ACCESSORIES

Every year there are more and more devices, gadgets and tools coming on to the gardening market. Some are innovative and useful, others not worth bothering with, but in the main, anything that makes gardening easier is worth trying. The trick is to look at them all and work out which ones you actually need.

WATERING

Whether or not our summers are getting drier and we are facing more water restrictions, it is in everyone's interest to use water more wisely. More and more accessories are being developed which will help with watering, either by making the water last longer (by conserving it) or helping deliver the water to the right spot, where the plants will benefit the most. Devices such as a porous pipe (a seep hose) are excellent for laying in borders and running at very low pressure to allow the water to gradually seep into the soil instead of evaporating from the surface.

If you have a lot of containers, it might be worth buying a 'spaghetti' watering system, whereby water is

Left Flower pouches can bring colour to unexpected places. Once the seedlings you plant in them have become established, the pouches can be hung on posts, fences and walls.

Below Seep hoses can be threaded around the garden to deliver water directly to the roots of plants, minimizing evaporation: a perfect low-maintenance device.

TIMERS

Watering plants in the evening or early morning allows them to make best use of the water, before the sun has a chance to evaporate it. To save you time, use a timing device that can switch the water supply to the hose on and off at the required moment, or to cut out after a certain amount of water has been delivered. Timers can be battery- or water-powered, and are very effective.

FLOWER BAGS AND POUCHES

Flower bags are plastic bags or tubes (usually coloured) that are filled with compost and have a series of planting holes in them, ready for receiving young plants. Pouches are netted bags of compost, which can be cut to plant seedlings. Both bags and pouches can be hung from a wall or fence to form a vertical display, and the tubes can even be wound around posts. They are ideal for bedding displays, and can be refilled and used for several seasons.

Designer accessories

Not all accessories need to be useful. Look out for decorative items, such as the shell below, to liven up functional areas of your garden, or use them tucked away in a corner to add an element of surprise. For extra interest, chimes introduce sound and movement and, if you're using metal ones in an area that catches the sun, there'll be a play of light on them, too.

delivered to each pot through a short, thin tube fed, in turn, by a larger tube from the tap. The water is delivered directly to the roots of the plant, so none is wasted as run-off from the foliage, and the supply can be turned off once the pots are moist.

NON-RETURN VALVE

This is an inexpensive gadget which fits on to an outside tap, between the tap and the hose pipe. It prevents any contaminated water from returning to the mains supply, should there be a sudden drop in pressure. In fact some water companies are now insisting that one of these is fitted when using a hose pipe.

Above Lawn sprinklers are useful for large areas of similar plants which are all growing at a similar rate. They are ideal for watering lawns, newly planted bedding schemes, or vegetable plots.

Right Garden ornaments, such as this snail shell, can also be functional. In this case it's collecting rain water, but it could be filled with grain to try and entice the birds away from young plants and seedlings.

HOW TO CHEAT
at gardening

Getting the best out of your garden doesn't always involve hard graft. With a few short cuts from the *Ground Force* experts, you can make it change size, look brighter and even acquire sudden antiquity. It's just a case of know-how.

AGEING AND DISTRESSING CONTAINERS

One of the main problems with any type of garden makeover is that, for a while, everything looks brand new, which, of course, it often is. To give the new garden a more established look, older plants or containers can be introduced, but this can be very costly. A cheaper alternative is to buy some relatively new items which can then be artificially aged or weathered. Terracotta and concrete pots can appear quite old in a matter of weeks by applying a coating of natural yoghurt to attract fungi, algae and lichen. These add a green patina to the surface and give the illusion of age.

MAKING THE SMALL SEEM BIGGER

Besides the techniques of path-laying on pages 38–41, and using soft colours at the end of a garden to make it seem longer, you can try diminishing sizes. By keeping tall structures near the house and smaller ones at the end, or gradually reducing the height of a wall, you might just create the illusion of space. Mirrors are highly effective space creators, giving a sense of looking through a window into another part of the garden. They are also useful for shady areas because, by positioning them correctly, light can be reflected, increasing the range of plants that can be grown.

You can also make walkways with a double hedge or avenue of trees appear longer by having the distance between the two lines of trees or hedging plants closer together at the furthest distance. This is known as the 'tram line' effect. Finally, statues or figures that are only two-thirds or half the height of life size, placed at the end of fairly short avenues or walkways, will make the distance appear much greater.

Plants with small leaves and flowers can also be used to create a sense of distance, especially if plants with larger leaves and flowers are used nearer the house. And in a garden that is almost square it is possible to make it appear longer and narrower by creating borders along the sides. The sense of distance is enhanced if you plant them with hot colours, and the end of the garden with cool ones.

Left Just as they do indoors, mirrors reflect their surroundings, creating an illusion of greater space. As illustrated here, they can also be used in shady areas of the garden to reflect light.

Right This is probably the nearest we'll ever get to Alice's experience through the looking-glass. The cleverly constructed trellis creates a *trompe l'oeil* effect, making the viewer feel drawn into the view reflected by the mirror.

HOW TO PUT UP MIRRORS AND *TROMPE L'OEIL*

1 Prepare eight timber battens (just larger than the dimensions of the mirror) by measuring and cutting them to the correct length. Drill four of them at regular intervals, making sure that the drill bit passes right through the wood. Place the four drilled battens against the wall and put a pencil through the holes to mark the wall behind. Using a masonry bit, drill holes into the wall and insert plastic or fibre screw plugs into the holes.

2 Fix the four battens to the wall – top, bottom and both sides – and nail or screw a plywood sheet to the battens. Fix one of the remaining four battens to the bottom batten already fixed to the wall, leaving a gap into which to slot the mirror into position. Screw two side battens through the edge of the backing to the plywood, and fasten the last batten into place at the top.

3 Add trellis to the wall around the mirror. This can be home-made or bought as a kit, and more battens can be fitted to the wall so that they radiate out from the mirror in a 'rising sun' arrangement.

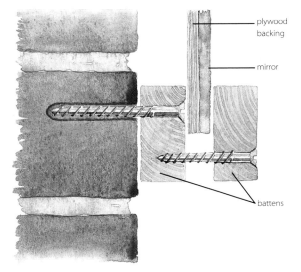

plywood backing

mirror

battens

Serpentine paths and lawns

One of the main problems of small gardens is that they proide only limited interest because the whole garden can be seen from a single point. By creating a serpentine lawn or winding path, the walk through the garden seems longer and makes it possible to divide the garden into several different sections.

useful addresses

Most materials and tools can be bought or hired from local garden centres, nurseries and hire shops, so it is best to try these first. Specific materials used in the programmes may be obtained from the following suppliers.

SUPPLIERS OF PLANTS

Architectural Plants
Cooks Farm
Nuthurst, Horsham
West Sussex
RH1 6LH
Tel. 01403 891772

Basingstoke Garden Centre
Winchester Road
North Waltham
Basingstoke, Hampshire
PG25 2DT
Tel. 01256 397155

Country Gardens Centres Ltd
Garden Centre
Roundabout
Bath Road
Thatcham, Berkshire
RG18 3AN
Tel. 01635 873700

Dobbies Garden World
Melville Garden Centre
Lasswade
Midlothian
EH18 1AZ
Tel. 0131 663 1941

Garden Style
Wrecclesham Hill
Farnham
Surrey
GU10 4JX
Tel. 01252 735331

Notcutts Garden Centre
Waterers Nurseries
London Road
Bagshot
Surrey
GU19 5DG
Tel. 01276 472288

Pantiles Nurseries Ltd
(for specialist plants and trees)
Almners Road
Lyne, Chertsey
Surrey
KT16 0BJ
Tel. 01932 872195

Rolawn Ltd
(for turf)
Elvington
York
YO41 4XR
Tel. 01904 608661

Tendercare Nurseries
Southlands Road
Denham
Uxbridge
Middlesex
UB9 4HD
Tel. 01895 835544

MACHINERY AND EQUIPMENT HIRE/SUPPLY

ATF Supplies (for bamboo canes, round poles, wattle fencing)
Foxcotte Barn
Foxcotte Lane
Charlton
Andover
Hampshire
SP10 4AB
Tel. 01264 366211

Awning World Ltd
5 Barrons Great Outdoors
Chapel Lane
Coppull
Chorley
Lancashire
PR7 4NJ
Tel. 01257 793008

Border Hardcore and Rockery Stone Company Ltd
(for cobbles)
Buttington Quarry
Buttington
Welshpool
Powys
SY21 8SZ
Tel. 01938 570375

Building Supplies Graham Group plc
96 Leeds Road
Huddersfield
West Yorkshire
HD1 4RH
Tel. 01484 537366
200 branches around the country

Catalan Classics
(for large pots)
The Maltings
Chelmsford Road
Norton Heath
Essex
CM4 0LN
Tel. 01277 824747

Cuprinol Paints
(for water-based paints)
Corixa Communications Ltd
1 Berkley Square
Bristol
BS8 1HL
Tel. 01179 493394

English Hurdle
(for rose arches and willow fencing)
Curload
Stokes St Gregory
Taunton
Somerset
TA3 6JD
Tel. 01823 698418

Erin-Gardena
(for water irrigation system)
Astonia House
High Street
Baldock
Hertfordshire
SG7 6PP
Tel. 01462 895511

Felco
(for secateurs and pruning equipment)
Burton McCall
163 Parker Drive
Leicester
LE4 0JP
Tel. 01162 340800

Forest Fencing Ltd
Stanford Court
Stanford Bridge
Near Worcester
Hereford and Worcestershire
WR6 6SR
Tel. 01886 812451

Harveys Sand and Gravel
(for rockery stone)
Unit 7
Bramble Close
Swindon
Wiltshire
SN2 6DW
Tel. 01793 643744

Hayter Mowers
Spellbrook
Bishop Stortford
Hertfordshire
CH23 4BU
Tel. 01279 723444

Hozelock Ltd (for garden lighting)
Waterslade House
Thame Road
Hadden Hame
Near Aylesbury
Buckinghamshire
HP17 8JD
Tel. 01844 294535

Husqvarna Forest and Garden UK
(for protective clothing and chainsaws)
Oldends Lane Industrial Estate
Stonedale Road
Stonehouse
Gloucestershire
GL10 3SY
Tel. 01453 820310

ITW Paslode (for nail gun)
Queensway
Fforestfach
Swansea, Gwent
SA5 4ED
Tel. 01792 589800

Jewsons Ltd
Southland House
Matlock Road
Coventry
West Midlands
CV1 4JQ
Tel. 0800 539766
400 branches around the country

Kerb-Line
(for turf-stripping machine)
20 Glamis Close
Oakley, Basingstoke
Hampshire
RG23 7NQ
Tel. 01256 781922

Marshalls Mono Ltd
(for paving)
Brier Lodge
Brookfoot, Southowram
Halifax, West Yorkshire
HX3 9SY
Tel. 01422 306300

Melcourt Industries Ltd
(for play bark)
Eight Bells House
Church Street
Tetbury
Gloucestershire
GL8 9JG
Tel. 01666 502711

Mill Water Gardens
(for water features)
Mead Mill
Mill Lane
Romsey
Hampshire
SO51 8EQ
Tel. 01794 513444

Mushroom Log Kit
Green Bank
Inverurie
Aberdeenshire
AB51 5AA
Tel. 01467 671315

Newbury Salvage Ltd
(for railway sleepers, sculptures)
Kelvin Road
Newbury
Berkshire
RG14 2DB
Tel. 01635 528120

Sampsons Fencing and Leisure Buildings
(for summerhouses)
Jarretts Garden Centre
Bath Road
Willsbridge
Bristol
BS15 6EF
Tel. 01179 329777

T. Chamber and Son Ltd
(for tanalized timber)
70–72 Leyton Road
Stratford
London
E15 1DG
Tel. 0181 534 6318

Town and Country Paving Ltd
(for terracotta tiles)
Unit 10
Shrublands Nurseries
Roundstone Lane
Angmering
West Sussex
BN16 4AT
Tel. 01903 776297

PROFESSIONAL ORGANIZATIONS

For a list of competent landscape contractors in your area, contact:

British Association of Landscape Industries (BALI)
9 Henry Street
Keighley
West Yorkshire
BD21 3DR
Tel. 01535 606139

Landscape Institute
6–7 Bernard Mews
London
SW11 1QU
Tel. 0171 738 9166

further reading

The Complete Book of the Water Garden
Philip Swindells and David Mason
Ward Lock
1995

The Complete First Time Gardener
Geoff Hamilton and Gay Search
BBC Worldwide
1996

The Complete Guide to Gardening with
Containers
Susan Berry and Steve Bradley
Collins and Brown
1995

Garden Structures
Richard Wiles
Mitchell Beazley
1994

Gardeners' World Border Planning
Anne Swithinbank
BBC Worldwide
1996

Gardeners' World Container Gardening
Anne Swithinbank
BBC Worldwide
1994

Gardeners' World The Garden Lovers' Guide
to Britain
Kathryn Bradley-Hole
BBC Worldwide
1998

Gardeners' World Practical Gardening Course
Geoff Hamilton
BBC Worldwide
Revised edition 1998

Gardeners' World Pocket Plant Guides:
Climbers (1997)
Hardy Perennials (1998)
Patio Plants (1998)
Plants for Shade (1997)
Roses (1997)
Summer Bedding (1997)
Water Garden Plants (1998)
Winter Colour (1997)
All by Andi Clevely
BBC Worldwide

Gardening from Scratch 1 and 2
Gay Search
BBC Worldwide
1996 and 1998

Gardening Techniques
Alan Titchmarsh
Mitchell Beazley
1995

Old Garden, New Gardener
Gay Search and Geoff Hamilton
BBC Worldwide
1995

The RHS Plant Finder
Chris Philip; ed. Tony Lord
Dorling Kindersley
1998

Step-by-step Outdoor Brickwork
Penny Swift
New Holland Publishers (UK)
1992

Step-by-step Outdoor Woodwork
Mike Lawrence
New Holland Publishers (UK)
1998

Step-by-step Town Gardens
Valerie Bradley
Lorenz Books
1998

picture references

BBC Books would like to thank the following for providing photographs and for permission to reproduce copyright material. While every effort has been made to trace and acknowledge all copyright holders, we would like to apologize should there have been any errors or omissions.

The **Garden Picture Library** (9t J.S. Sira), (23r, 28 Brigitte Thomas), (30, 101 Mel Watson), (36l, 38, 48, 62, 76t, 78, 79, 108, 112l, 113r, 116, 123 Ron Sutherland), (39l, 81r, 92, 95r, 97 Steve Wooster), (43, 105b Lamontagne), (52 Gil Hanly), (61l, 71, 102 John Baker), (70t Sunniva Harte), (72t, 94l, 98, 100t, 104, 110, 114b, 120l John Glover), (80l, 82 Jane Legate), (88 Juliette Wade), (96t Juliet Greene), (99t Henk Oijkman), (103b Lynne Brotchie), (106 A l Lord), (107b Friedrich Strauss), (112r, 117b Linda Burgess), (113l, 118 Emma Peios), (119 Howard Rice), (120r Andrea Jones); **John Glover** 6r, 20t, 50l, 58; **Jerry Harpur** 47t, 107t; **Holt Studios** 55b; **Horticultural Picture Library** 23l, 25l; **Kerb-Line** 16b; **Photos Horticultural** 56, 64, 70b, 74, 94r, 109, 117t; **Harry Smith** 54, 55t, 66, 68, 95l, 100b, 105t

Photographs © BBC (2, 6l, 7l, 9b, 13, 15, 24, 25r, 37l, 45, 47b, 51l, 59t, 61r, 67t, 77, 80r, 81l, 83, 85b, 114t, 115b, 122 John Glover), (5, 16t, 36r, 37r, 39r, 40, 44, 57, 60r, 76b, 99b Susan Bell), (17, 121t Tim Sandall), (22l, 32, 33t, 35t, 89, 90b, 91, 93, 111 Jo Whitworth), (26t, 49, 85t William Shaw), (35b Eric Crichton), (69 Stephen Hamilton). All other photographs © BBC/Craig Easton.

index